S0-CEY-102

WHITE PAPERS OF AN
OUTRAGED CONSERVATIVE

By the same author

THE INDESTRUCTIBLE IRISH
THE KEY

WHITE PAPERS OF AN OUTRAGED CONSERVATIVE

John Philip Cohane

THE BOBBS-MERRILL COMPANY, INC.

INDIANAPOLIS   NEW YORK

The Bobbs-Merrill Company, Inc.
Publishers: Indianapolis / New York
Copyright © 1972 by John Philip Cohane
All rights reserved
Library of Congress catalog card number 72–190112
Designed by Jack Jaget
Manufactured in the United States of America

Those who forget history are condemned to relive it.
—GEORGE SANTAYANA

To three who have not forgotten history:
Kingman Brewster, Jr., president, Yale University
U.S. Senator William Proxmire of Wisconsin
James Reston, vice president, the New York *Times*

1

If we just go ahead as we are,
extermination is inevitable.

—Dr. George Wald

ALL MY adult life, a period of some forty years, I have
regarded myself as a political conservative in the literal
sense of the term, a "moderate" who is anxious to preserve
the traditional American way of life. I usually found myself
in the middle of the road on most national issues and at
election time often swung back and forth, voting one time
for a Democrat, the next time for a Republican, depending
on the political climate and the qualifications of the candidates.

For the past decade, however, and especially during the
Nixon-Agnew Administration, I have found myself increasingly disturbed and finally outraged at the trend of American
affairs, both domestic and foreign. Time and again it seemed
that words were being said and actions taken that ran directly counter to what I had been taught were the principles
on which the American republic was founded. The nation
appeared to be working itself into a situation from which it
would be more and more difficult to return to what I had

always believed was true democracy. In early 1971 I found myself wholeheartedly in agreement with Dr. George Wald, 1967 Nobel Prize winner in physiology and professor of biology at Harvard University, when he declared before a gathering of scientists in California: "If we just go ahead as we are, extermination is inevitable." By comparison with the 1930s, Dr. Wald continued, "The times are much worse now. At least we knew in the depths of the Depression that it would not last forever. Now we don't know that our situation isn't permanent. I don't see any way out of it. Things are going to get ever so much worse before they can get any better."

The root of our problems, stated Dr. Wald, lies in the abandonment of founding principles, in the gradual weaving into the fabric of American society of the evils our fore-fathers came to this continent to avoid in Europe.

As a middle-aged member of what appears to be not a silent but a shell-shocked majority, I have had experiences during the past few years I never thought could happen: A prominent London publisher, temperate in his views and habits, with a background of twenty years working in the United States, declared flatly to me, "America has become everything it started out *not* to be." And I found myself without strong confuting arguments.

A pleasant, ruddy-cheeked, comfortable woman in her sixties—the granddaughter of a distinguished savant, a dis-ciple of Henry George—gazed out at the early-summer Connecticut landscape and said calmly, "It may horrify you to hear me say this, but personally I think the only solution to our problems is to blow up the ghettos of America and everybody in them with atom bombs. Those heroin addicts. The whole lot."

A former Yale classmate who, for several million dollars, sold his regional business a few years ago to a national manu-facturer fingered a bacardi cocktail and commented on the possible nomination of Senator Edward Kennedy for the

Presidency: "If he gets it, there's only one thing to do to him. The same thing that was done to his two brothers. I don't give a damn whether a Democrat or a Republican wins so long as he's not a liberal."

The wife of a well-known Wall Street broker declared that the assassination of Martin Luther King was "the greatest thing that's happened in the last ten years."

Driving along back roads through New England one late Sunday afternoon, past immaculate split-level ranch-type houses surrounded by neatly manicured lawns, interspersed with snow-white steepled colonial churches, eighteenth-century clapboard farmhouses, town centers like children's cardboard cutouts, neo-classical service stations bedecked with American flags, on into the stifling, rubble-strewn outskirts of the Bronx, I suddenly realized fully that the United States had already created its own unheralded, unabashed form of apartheid.

One becomes engulfed in an ever-mounting flood of half-truths, innuendos, perversions and distortions coming from the highest offices of the land. The New York *Times* of January 1, 1970, announced that the Vice President of the United States had been chosen by the International Press Institute in Zurich as "the most serious threat to the freedom of information in the western world in 1969." Abraham Lincoln said: "He who makes an assertion without knowing whether it is true or false is guilty of falsehood, and the accidental truth of the assertion does not justify or excuse him."

Some on the perimeter of the American scene believe that the only way to cure the nation's ills is to move drastically in the direction of socialism or communism. Others on the opposite side of the perimeter have their own pet totalitarian ideas as to what is needed. One group or the other, perhaps both, may be right. Personally I don't think so. At any rate this is no handbook for extremists. It is a suggestion that other middle-of-the-road Americans take a long look at where they stand at this critical juncture, decide whether or not they like what they see and then decide what, if anything, they want to do about the present state of affairs. It is toward this broad group that these words are especially directed. For it is they who are in the gravest danger of losing the very things they are most anxious to preserve.

As one sifts through the headline-making events since World War II, examines the first 160 years of American history against this later period and searches behind recent spectacular violence and erupting tensions for the complicated, ubiquitous reasons for such violence and tensions, there emerges a long list of underlying causes for what George Wald has termed a "crisis of crises." Those who keep abreast of the news are familiar with many or most of them. What is staggering in my opinion is to see them all assembled in one place, to examine the relationship between them and to try to determine how and why they came into existence. It has been said that the American people have a good "forgetter," and this is especially true when the air rings with a bewildering assortment of claims and counterclaims.

Twice before in this century the American people lifted themselves out of lesser bogs of despair—during the Roosevelt-Wilson era prior to World War I and during the FDR years between the 1929 crash and World War II. Perhaps, as Nicholas Machiavelli observed some centuries ago, "To ensure a long existence to religious sects or republics it is necessary frequently to bring them back to their original principles."

2

> The hammers that destroyed the
> temple were forged in the temple.
>
> —ANATOLE FRANCE

I WAS brought up in a rough school, the same one attended by star pupils Richard Milhous Nixon, Spiro T. Agnew, Lydon Baines Johnson and countless others of a highly ambitious, hard-driving generation. I was nurtured on Horatio Alger, Frank Merriwell, Stover at Yale, Tom Swift, *Boy's Life* and *The American Boy,* such meaty fare as *The Americanization of Edward Bok,* George Horace Latimer's *Letters from a Self-Made Merchant to His Son*—America's answer to Lord Chesterfield which ran through thirty-five editions between 1903 and 1941—and a special favorite, James Burnley's *Millionaires and Kings of Enterprise,* in which one meets Hiram Stevens Maxim of Piscataquis County, Maine, who bequeathed to posterity the automatic machine gun. In one respect Maxim was premature. He moved to England, became a partner in Vickers Sons and Maxim and was knighted, all because he decided that "America is not a fighting country; they will only require about twenty machine guns a year." Those who think our children are not being educated as well as we were should spend a few hours with Messrs. Latimer and Burnley.

Before I was twelve I was the scourge of our placid New England neighborhood. Housewives hanging up clothes or chatting with friends ducked indoors when they saw me coming. I was out after school hours hawking subscriptions to *The Saturday Evening Post,* leatherbound editions of *Elbert Hubbard's Scrapbook,* tubes of iron-rust remover, packets of bluing. Sometimes I didn't understand the purpose of the product I was selling, training which sharpened my creative talents for the years ahead. Every Saturday morning I hauled crisp copies of the *Weekend Shopping News* house to house in an express wagon. My first venture into advertising came when I distributed prescription blanks bearing my eye-physician father's name and office address to every front door within a five-block radius of our home.

My early teen-age years were consumed during school terms "going out" for everything in sight—athletics, editorships, managerial posts—during vacation months cutting lawns, giving swimming lessons, collecting tickets at country-club movies, selling socks and ties in a department store before Christmas, working for three summers as a reporter on an evening newspaper. As my hunger grew by what it fed on, the pace became hotter and more competitive at Yale, where through assiduously working on five publications I earned more money during senior year than any other University undergraduate in America. My parents were proud of me. I was proud of myself.

And yet even in those bright college years all was not as portrayed in the lives of Dink Stover and Frank Merriwell. It was a bit of a shock, for example, to discover that cheating on exams and in classes was run-of-the-mill at Yale. Everybody did it, so you did it yourself. It was the first step toward the conclusion that more mischief is plotted against America in its golf clubs than in its ghettos, that our traditional values have been and are being destroyed by their self-appointed protectors, not from outside but from within, not from the bottom up but from the top down—a process directly opposite to "subversion." Oscar Wilde said: "For each man kills the thing he loves." And Anatole France: "The hammers that destroyed the temple were forged in the temple." Both statements are relevant if out of their original context.

There was a second connecting link in the golf-club–ghetto chain at Yale, another tiny cause of the gigantic effect that now looms like Dr. Frankenstein's creation before middle-aged, disbelieving, uncomprehending eyes, another step toward the present situation in which for our leaders to try to force the American people back into a 1920 stratified, authoritative society from which they have partially escaped is like trying to stuff a raging tiger into a battered bird cage. This was the again disillusioning but gracefully lived-with fact that at Yale in the 1930s free elections didn't exist, any more than they exist today in many of the countries the United States is supporting, any more than the American people had a free choice of opposites in the 1968 Presidential election. Everything at Yale was run by "packs." Fraternity elections, positions on publications, class officers, managerships, even some team captaincies—the entire undergraduate "honorary" structure was rigged.

It was an ingenious system that had flourished for some ten or fifteen years. Three or four men who were badly wanted by a fraternity would pick sixteen or seventeen friends and they would all go in convoy-fashion, the weak with the strong, as a pack. Or, of nine board members of a publication, five would secretly get together and agree to vote one another into pre-selected offices. The four outside the pack never realized what had happened. Many extremely capable students went unrewarded throughout their college careers.

Those in the know at Yale soon learned one all-important fact: It isn't *how* you get where you get that counts. It's *where* you get that counts. It was a lesson swiftly applied to conditions after college. Many a prominent Old Eli has risen to fame and fortune by keeping his eyes glued to that key fact. Nor has it been a lesson confined to the campus at New Haven. It has been a countrywide basic principle that has seeped through and rotted the upper structure of American public and business life.

By the mid-1930s, with Wall Street a shambles after the 1929 carnage, many hot-eyed young men clutching diplomas who ten years earlier would have become bond salesmen hopefully headed for Madison Avenue. I was eagerly and happily among them. During the next few decades we helped litter the landscape with beer bottles and cans, deodorant receptacles, hair sprays, toothpaste tubes, worn-out automobiles, discarded rubber tires, soft-drink containers, cigarette butts, chewing-gum wrappers, empty packages of breakfast cereals, dog foods, baby foods, cat foods, soap flakes and powders, headache remedies, depilatories, laxatives, corn removers, stomach settlers, tranquilizers, denture cleaners, face creams, hand creams, skin creams, shaving creams, sleeping pills, Tampax, Kotex, Kleenex, toilet paper, trading stamps, DDT cans, gin and whiskey bottles, broken-down radios, TV sets, power lawnmowers, refrigerators, cooking ranges, electric razors, outboard motors. Today's delights became tomorrow's debris. What T. S. Eliot described as a nation of "concrete highways and lost golf balls" was being slowly buried up to the armpits in discarded junk.

My generation entered advertising just as the wooden nutmeg salesmen, the con men, the itinerant peddlers, the patent-medicine vendors, the carnival and sideshow barkers, the hawkers, hucksters and hustlers who had plied their somewhat disreputable trade ever since Revolutionary days were starting to scramble up into the big-time. Moving into spacious, smartly furnished air-conditioned offices behind shiny façades, perfecting an impressive pseudo-scientific jargon, advertising men—with the rapid growth of mass media and correspondingly larger revenues—became semi-respectable. With our bright, alert faces, crew haircuts, conventionally tailored Brooks Brothers uniforms we added considerably to the aura. But it never became what you could honestly call a profession.

During my first few months in advertising, becoming increasingly obvious all through twenty-five turbulent, intensely exciting years, one cardinal principle emerged which has always dominated advertising and which still reigns supreme. It is the all-important yardstick applied to any consumer message: Don't worry whether it's true or not. Will it sell? This underlying philosophical principle, or lack of principle, has not only raised havoc in the consumer-goods field but has sent American affairs spinning downward at home and abroad during the past ten years. Armed with highly polished techniques, versed in the use of mass communications, the ad men have carried their tawdry will-it-sell? banner into the political and civic arenas, turning it over to those who are in precarious control of the nation's destiny. True "control," if it can be called that, rests with a collectively mindless, inadequately directed public-influence monster that has plunked itself squarely down in the driver's seat and is zigzagging along a road toward ever more unpleasant situations and problems. The American people, who successfully resisted the frontal blandishments of the Father Coughlins, Huey Longs and Joe McCarthys, are now being had from all bewildering directions. In an atmosphere burbling with hypocrisy and lies, cynicism is rampant; values good and bad are topsy-turvy. The compass spins crazily without polarization. All the way from trying to persuade us to put dubious drug products and questionable foods into our stomachs to urging young men to lay down their lives in Indochina, the key will-it-sell? principle and the employed techniques are the same. *Caveat emptor* has never had more profound or sinister significance than today, whether someone is trying to sell us war, God, anti-communism or a new, improved deodorant. Deceit is the accepted order of the hour. Confidence in what the country's leaders are saying and doing is being eroded. Educators, legislators, the news media—aware of what is taking place—are being told in brazen, unsubtle language to sit down, shut up and tend to their own business.

This is the most outrageous facet of all. The advice that has been given, the warnings that have been sounded by some of the nation's most respected citizens, including many highly placed Republicans, including one former Republican President of the United States, are being distorted into the "hollow rhetoric" of "radical liberals." Even the word "priority"—once a favorite of President Nixon himself—has been labeled suspect. Underneath the surface of this biggest of big lies the record of what has been said as to how the country's ills can best be cured is clear for all to see who wish to see.

3

No mortal skill can make military power effective on democratic principles. A democratic people can perhaps carry on a war longer and better than any others; because no other can so well comprehend the object, raise the means, or bear the sacrifices. But these sacrifices include the surrender, for the time being, of the essential principles of the government. Personal independence in the soldier, like personal liberty in the civilian, must be waived for the preservation of the nation. With shipwreck staring men in the face, the choice lies between despotism and anarchy, trusting to the common sense of those concerned, when the danger is over, to revert to the old safeguards. It is precisely because democracy is an advanced stage in human society, that war, which belongs to a less advanced stage, is peculiarly inconsistent with its habits.

—THOMAS WENTWORTH HIGGINSON

THE ABOVE passage which appears in an essay, "Regular Volunteer Officers," was written by a Unitarian clergyman from Massachusetts who served as a colonel of the 1st South Carolina Regiment in the Civil War. It sums up in terms pertinent to the present the dangers that beset a democratic society in time of war. During the past quarter century democracy in America has been struggling to survive in an intensely warlike climate—the actual fighting of wars, the constant dread of all-out war, the feverish preparations for such a war. The traditional American system of government has been subjected to enormous pressures from many directions.

President Eisenhower in his 1961 farewell address to the nation—a remarkable speech delivered unfortunately at the end, not the beginning, of his political career and almost totally ignored by those who followed him—paraphrased Higginson's words of a century earlier in more immediate terms: "In the councils of government, we must guard against the acquisition of unwarranted influence, whether sought or unsought, by the military/industrial complex. The potential rise of misplaced power exists and will persist." Carrying this a step further, the departing Chief Executive warned: "There will always be crises ahead, foreign and domestic, but the real dangers lie not in the exigencies themselves but in the means chosen for meeting them."

During these troubled times an alarming cleavage has taken place within the nation, a sharp division between those who share the views of Higginson and Eisenhower that the *means* must at all times be wisely and carefully chosen and those who think certain *ends* must be attained no matter what means are used. Under duress the very principles at stake have become blurred and are often lost sight of.

Hedley Donovan, editor-in-chief of *Time,* in an article, "Who Is America? What Are We All About?" which appeared in the April 1969 issue of *Fortune,* draws a graphic picture of the widening gulf between what Americans believed during the early days and what they believe today. He contends there is a "loss of a working consensus, for the first time in our lives, as to what we think America means in the world and to the world." Donovan points out that in the beginning our predecessors affirmed their faith in the United States with a fervor that was religious in its intensity.

John Adams wrote that it was the design of Providence to use America for the "illumination" and "emancipation" of all mankind. Thomas Jefferson maintained that "God led our forefathers as Israel of old" and called America "the world's best hope." Abraham Lincoln, during the Civil War, went a step further and declared it "the last best hope on earth." George Bancroft, the great scholar trained at Harvard, Heidelberg and Göttingen, died an old man in the 1890s firmly convinced that our history was "the story of the wonder-working of the hand of God in the American forest."

But, *Time's* editor-in-chief continues, in the 1920s "for Americans who did still have faith in the God of their fathers it was hard to believe that the spreading of the urban industrial landscape could enjoy quite the same divine favor as the crossing of the continental divide. And if anything of the old idea of the chosen people had survived the 1920s, the Great Depression of the 1930s certainly did not help it. Now for a large, literate, democratic society once to have held so strongly such a righteous and spacious view of itself, and then in a few years to lose it, should be a profoundly unsettling experience."

Donovan believes that the "35-year crisis—from the rearming of Nazi Germany, starting in 1935, through World War II, through Korea and the cold war, through Vietnam" —has in one sense postponed our facing up to ourselves and the discrepancies between what we believe and what we do, by sustaining us with the conviction that in all our struggles —against fascism and communism alike—we have been battling for democracy on a worldwide basis. In spite of this powerful cohesive belief, however, during this same long, seemingly endless period since 1935, a period during which we have been constantly torn apart by the schizophrenic conflict between "military power" and "democratic principles" so aptly described by Thomas Wentworth Higginson, we have obviously lost a great deal more than we have gained as far as eroded and confused values are concerned. We were innocent, starry-eyed babes-in-the-wood back in the mid-1930s compared to what we are now. Certainly students, educators, publishers, editors and writers like Hedley Donovan, other professionals and a host of political figures as well as many rational elders, have increasingly for some time been regarding with worry, often with cynicism and hopelessness, occasionally with horror as when confronted by such episode as the My Lai massacre, much of what fate, ourselves, and/or God hath wrought.

As we approach the 200th anniversary of the founding of the Republic, we cannot survey the landscape in any direction without being, to say the least, profoundly disturbed. First, and perhaps most important of all, we as a nation have been and are more and more acting as though we are, again in Higginson's terms, men "with shipwreck staring us in the face," men who must choose between "despotism and anarchy, *trusting to the common sense of those concerned, when the danger is over, to revert to the old safeguards.*" And every month, against our own common sense, we are being shoved into corners where we must choose one or the other of these all-or-nothing extreme postures— despotism or anarchy.

The fear of communism and a vicious treadmill of Gross National Product, profits and payrolls has resulted in a bill for weapons of war and assorted related items and services that has hit the staggering total of close to $80 billion a year, up nearly 70 percent from 1961 when Eisenhower left office warning us of the dangers inherent in the fact that the U.S. for the first time had a *"permanent arms industry"* on which we spend annually "more than the net income of all United States corporations."

In *The Military Establishment* (Harper & Row, 1970), Adam Yarmolinsky points out that the U.S. defense budget "accounts for more than two-thirds of the Federal government's purchases of goods and services." Mr. Yarmolinsky explores in depth "the impact of the military establishment on the system of national values; the problem of moral callousness in war, and the concept of national guilt," with his final sentence sounding the ominous warning: "If the United States is to avoid becoming a militarized society, the public and its civilian representatives must retain the ultimate right of decision on such central political issues as counter-revolution and insurgency, war and peace."

There are those who will argue convincingly that we have *already* become just such a militarized society, one which, due to the strength of its tough-minded proponents, will become increasingly difficult to reshape. Senator J. William Fulbright has warned against the "arrogance of power," but were the right people listening? All of the candidates in the 1968 Presidential election proclaimed "We cannot become the world's policeman," but are we not? Arnold Toynbee has called us the "most dangerous force on the planet" and many will not deny him.

Each month from the long-term view it becomes more obvious that the future of not only the United States but the whole world depends on a major breakthrough taking place in the arms race that has overshadowed all other issues since 1945. From the short-term view there is ample evidence that the waste, inefficiency, big profits, graft and corruption that always characterize huge expenditures on weapons permeate the American scene, exert an enormous and destructive influence on our political life and, as far as a high percentage of the population is concerned, stand in the way of attaining truly worthwhile peacetime goals. *Fortune,* in its August 1, 1969, issue devoted almost exclusively to defense, stated editorially:

> At staggering cost, the military has repeatedly bought weapons and deployed forces in ways that have added only mar-

ginally to national security. . . . [I]n the procurement of new weapons, both the military and its corporate suppliers have been guilty of wasteful practices and flagrantly disingenuous cost estimates. . . .

For a long time, and particularly since the departure of the Eisenhower Administration, few of the outside checks and balances that constrain other federal agencies have been applied to the military establishment.

It is true that the interplay between the services and their suppliers generates pressures to maintain high levels of defense spending, *almost irrespective of the external threat.* The natural desire of military men to have ever more sophisticated and expensive weaponry coincides with the desire of contractors to supply it. . . .

Unless brought under control, [present trends] can easily drive the defense budget to more than $100 billion within a few years. [The Joint Chiefs each year for the past few years have requested] an annual budget in excess of $105 billion. . . . No President since five-star general Eisenhower has been successful in forcing major reductions in the defense budget over their [generals and admirals] ceaseless warnings of imminent peril. [Italics added.]

As for what happens if and when our involvement in Indochina does end, Melvin Laird, Secretary of Defense under Nixon, has categorically stated: "Even if we are successful in eliminating the war in Vietnam, we are still not going to come up with a drastically reduced defense budget. . . . A drastically reduced defense budget will not provide adequate security in the world in which we live."

Pointing up the extent to which America has already become a "militarized" society, how completely saturated the U. S. economy is by a "permanent armaments industry," *Fortune* states that in 1968 the Defense Department awarded contracts to more than 23,000 companies. Two-thirds of prime contracts were for at least $1 million; the other one-third were worth over $10 million apiece. Although other states received larger over-all amounts, Connecticut topped the per-capita list with $805 for every man, woman and child in the state—a total of more than $1.8 billion. That the continuation of a high-powered weapons industry—aside from considerations of national defense—is of vital concern to a great many pocketbooks becomes distressingly obvious.

Fortune, turning to the world armaments race, reports that "the Institute for Strategic Studies in London in April 1969 completed a worldwide survey of military power and concluded: 'The Soviet Union now must be treated as a full equal [of America] in terms of strategic power and of her ability to control conflict in the developing worlds.'" An accompanying chart in America's leading business publication showed:

USA		USSR
3,487,000	men under arms	3,470,000
1,054	ICBMs	1,035
3,700	jet fighters	3,700

"The American lead in submarine-based missiles (656 to 129) and in long-range bombers (640 to 155)," continued the study, "is offset somewhat by the Soviet Union's 750 medium-ranged missiles and 1,050 medium bombers." The institute noted in passing that both countries were feeling the strain in terms of "general backwardness."

A study completed in the spring of 1971 by the same organization, generally accepted as the most reliable source for such figures, revealed that the United States and the USSR were maintaining parity, with stockpiling continuing on both sides. The full implications of this situation in which the national security of each country is being drastically *reduced* with each spiraling upward in the number and effectiveness of nuclear weapons will be discussed in a later chapter.

When one gets a peek behind the curtain at what is going on in the sale of new and obsolete arms to foreign nations, the impression of wasteful confusion, of inefficiency and large profits is particularly disturbing. Senator William Proxmire of Wisconsin, a senior member of the Senate Appropriations Committee, described the action vividly during a spring 1971 joint Congressional economics subcommittee meeting with representatives of the Defense Department:

> The problem here seems to be that no one is in charge. In some respects, the United States has been transformed from the arsenal of democracy to a gigantic discount supermarket with no check-out counters, no cash registers, no store managers—only clerks who blithely deliver to foreign governments . of practically any political persuasion whatever they happen to see or like. For most of the stuff there is no charge and no return.

Senator Proxmire complained that the Defense Department was "understating" the cost of military aid to foreign countries and thus "misleading" members of Congress. Although President Nixon's budget message listed only $625 *million* under military assistance, a study made for Proxmire's subcommittee by the General Accounting Office showed that the actual figure was about $5 *billion,* nearly eight times the amount shown in the Presidential budget.

Confirming widespread suspicion that armaments profits are running a great deal higher than admitted (a suspicion that prompted Senator George McGovern to urge unsuccessfully in 1969 that an "excess war profits tax" be enacted), another General Accounting Office story was leaked out to *Time* and the Washington *Post* during the first week of March 1971. To quote from Time:

"The report contains startling disparities between the pretax profits that defense and space contractors acknowledged in reply to a GAO questionnaire and the GAO's findings after a detailed study of 146 recently completed contracts totaling $4,256,000,000. This is how they compared:

PRETAX PROFITS	REPLY TO QUESTIONNAIRE	GAO STUDY OF 146 CONTRACTS
As a percentage of costs	3.9%	6.9%
As a return on total capital	10.2%	28.3%
As a return on equity capital	19.8%	56.1%

"By comparison, the pretax profits of all U.S. manufacturing corporations in 1969 averaged 20.1% on stockholders' equity. The results of the GAO study of the 146 contracts carries the strong implication that the average profit of 56.1% applies to most other defense contracts as well. The GAO claims that defense work is so lucrative because of a device that often removes much of the risk from Pentagon contracting: progress payments, made weekly, for up to 90% of the costs incurred. Progress payments rose from $3.3 billion in 1964 to $10 billion last year. Such payments are a common practice in business, particularly in construction. They amount to interest-free loans that enable contractors to operate almost entirely on the customers' money. In addition, defense contractors often use Government plants and equipment. As of 1967, the Government owned $2.6 billion worth of industrial production machinery; of that amount, 84% was used by 15 companies, including nine of the largest military contractors.

"Who is right? 'In general,' says the report, 'the higher the costs, the higher the profits,' because most Pentagon contracts are cost-plus. There is not much incentive for a company to invest in modern equipment, since greater efficiency might well lower both costs and profits. The report concludes that the amount of capital a company risks should be taken into account when the Pentagon negotiates a contract."

On the same day that Senator Proxmire was painting his dismal picture of the U.S. arms traffic with other countries, Secretary of Defense Melvin Laird, at a banquet in the Bangkok residence of the Prime Minister of Thailand, was reported in the nation's press as having told assembled members of the Asian government that U.S. military aid would "increase over the next ten years." This increased aid would be made available from "excess stocks of U.S. military equipment." (Current aid to Thailand runs to about $75 million a year.) Such an assurance, coupled with the Defense Secretary's statement that the end of the war in Vietnam will not "materially affect" the size of the U.S. defense budget, sets one pondering over a particular passage in President Nixon's message to Congress on domestic needs, delivered on April 14, 1969: "Peace has been the first priority. It concerns the future of civilization; and even in terms of our domestic needs themselves, what we will be able to do will depend in large measure on the prospects for an early end to the war in Vietnam."

No matter what happens to the war in Vietnam, it appears as though it will be a long time before sufficient funds are available to cope successfully with the problems confronting the nation at home.

4

> When in man's long history other great civilizations fell,
> it was less often from external assault than from internal
> decay. While serious external dangers remain, the gravest
> threats today are internal: haphazard urbanization, racial
> discrimination, disfiguring of the environment,
> unprecedented interdependence, the dislocation of human
> identity and motivation created by an affluent society—
> all resulting in a rising tide of individual and group
> violence. The greatness and durability of most
> civilizations has been finally determined by how they have
> responded to these challenges from within.
> —Report of the President's Commission on the Causes
> and Prevention of Violence, December 12, 1969

THE QUOTATION above is from the final report of the commission. Dr. Milton Eisenhower and his associates then closed shop and, like a number of early Nixon advisers, were no longer heard from. Elsewhere in this classic document the question of what would happen once the war in Vietnam ended was given special attention:

> We recognize that substantial amounts of funds cannot be
> transferred from sterile war purposes to more productive ones
> until our participation in the Vietnam War is ended. We also
> recognize that to make our society free of poverty and dis-

crimination, and to make our sprawling urban areas fit to inhabit, will cost a great deal of money and take a great deal of time. We believe, however, that we can and should make a major decision now to reassess our national priorities by placing these objectives in the first rank of the nation's goal.

Lost in the swirl of dramatic events and bursts of rhetoric during the past decade, ignored as blithely as President Eisenhower's last official advice and this report of the commission headed by his brother, are some of the finest declarations on American principles and purposes ever written. On the Democratic side of the fence no one has consistently made more common sense than Senator Fulbright of Arkansas. His warnings on the pitfalls involved in trying to keep both "war" and "peace" expenditures simultaneously going full tilt are far more significant and just as ignored today as they were back in 1966 and 1967:

> The war in Southeast Asia has affected the internal life of the United States in two important ways: It has diverted our energies from the Great Society program which began so promisingly a year ago, and it has generated the beginnings of a war fever in the minds of the American people and their leaders. . . . There is a kind of madness in the facile assumption that we can raise the many billions of dollars necessary to rebuild our schools and cities and public transports and eliminate the pollution of air and water while also spending tens of billions of dollars to finance an open-ended war in Asia. . . . America is showing some signs of that fatal presumption, that over-extension of power and mission, which brought ruin to ancient Athens, to Napoleonic France, and to Nazi Germany. The process has hardly begun, but the war we are now fighting can only accelerate it. If the war goes on and expands, if that fatal process continues to accelerate until America becomes what it is not and never has been, a seeker after unlimited power and empire, then Vietnam will have had a mighty and tragic fallout indeed.

The above is from a speech delivered on April 18, 1966. In a speech delivered during a Senate debate on December 3, 1967, Fulbright said: "More and more our economy, our Government, and our universities are adapting themselves to the requirements of continuing war—total war, limited war, and cold war." As the result of the dependence for orders, jobs, political favors on a defense budget of $75 billion, industrialists, businessmen, workers and politicians have "joined together in a military-industrial complex which has become a powerful new force for the perpetuation of foreign and military commitments, for the introduction and expansion of expensive new weapons systems, and as a result for the militarization of large segments of our national life."

It is an ironic situation—a Democratic Senator savagely maligned for sounding the same warning as Republican President Eisenhower. During the last week of February 1971 one found the "kind of madness in the facile assumption" that we can spend simultaneously billions on peacetime pursuits and tens of billions on war and defense finally coming home to roost on the White House steps. President Nixon, having just presented a self-styled "Keynesian" budget which proposed to do both jobs, ran head on into his own appointee to the chairmanship of the Federal Reserve System. Dr. Arthur Burns testified before Congress that the Nixon program would be "intolerably inflationary." Dr. Burns repeated his warning with equal emphasis in June 1971—shortly after which the international dollar crisis exploded.

The disastrous effects on a large segment of the American public caused by the failure of the Nixon Administration to "reassess national priorities" were dramatically highlighted in a report released by the Special Senate Committee on the Aging early in 1971. Housing conditions for the elderly have now reached "emergency proportions and demand immediate and far-reaching attention on all fronts." One-quarter of all Americans over sixty-five live in poverty. And the number is rapidly increasing—up 500,000 between 1968 and 1969 to 4,800,000. The committee blames "rising consumer prices, growing unemployment, larger medical costs, higher property taxes, inadequate pensions and the increase in the number of the aged. The economic problems of old age are not only unsolved for today's elderly, but they will not be solved for the elderly of the future—today's workers —unless the nation takes positive, comprehensive actions going far beyond those of recent years."

One feels that President Nixon, like Prince Haroun Al Rashid, should don a disguise and go out among the people for a few evenings with some of his intimates, observing at first hand how they are faring. And yet would their eyes see what is to be seen? Would they feel what should be felt? James Reston, in an April 1971 New York *Times* column, threw two scenes into juxtaposition that make you wonder.

1.)   President Nixon in the library of the White House being TV-interviewed by Howard K. Smith of ABC under a portrait of George Washington:

MR. SMITH: "How are you feeling these days?"

THE PRESIDENT: "Well, I don't feel it is the winter of my discontent. I suppose I keep it somewhat in perspective. . . . There are grave problems confronting America, but I am rather confident about the solution to those problems."

2.)   The mayors of America's biggest cities meeting with reporters in the Georgetown house of Katherine Graham, publisher of the Washington *Post*:

MAYOR JOHN LINDSAY OF NEW YORK: "The cities of America are in a battle for survival. . . . In New York we have a deficit this year of $300 million and face a deficit next year of $400 million. Frankly, even with help in Washington, I'm not sure we can pull out of the urban crisis in time."

MAYOR JOSEPH ALIOTO OF SAN FRANCISCO: "I'll be frank with you. The sky's falling in on us in the cities; it really is. . . . We need jobs and money for the poor and haven't either. Our people are trying to put a Maginot Line around the suburbs and zone them. We can't go on like this. Even the capitalistic system's not going to survive the way we're going."

MAYOR KENNETH GIBSON OF NEWARK: "Wherever the cities are going, Newark's going to get there first. We have the worst infant mortality, maternity mortality and crime rate in the country. We have 11 percent unemployed. If we had a bubonic plague in Newark everybody would try to help, but we really have a worse plague and nobody notices."

MAYOR WESLEY UHLMAN OF SEATTLE: "The old, the poor and the black can't leave the city because of poverty. We have 12.7 percent unemployed, and a class of the 'new unemployed'—professional men with a couple of degrees and nobody wants them. My brother's one of them. . . . We are suffering from a real sickness, a kind of schizophrenia. The people say they love the cities but wouldn't want to live there."

MAYOR MOON LANDRIES OF NEW ORLEANS: "It's not that we don't have enough money to rebuild; we don't have enough to give things a new coat of paint. The cities are going down the pipe, and if we're going to save them, we'd better do it now; three years from now will be too late."

MAYOR PETER FLAHERTY OF PITTSBURGH: "You can't understand how lonely a mayor feels with his problems. The people in the suburbs use our facilities but won't help pay for them."

MAYOR ROMAN GRIBBS OF DETROIT: "Our unemployment is now 14 percent. Our deficit is $83 million. . . . Last year we got $5 million in revenue from the state, but Michigan's now $100 million in the red."

Mr. Reston concluded:

All are for revenue-sharing but there is not enough revenue to share. Even if the President's revenue-sharing bill were passed, New York's share would add only 2% to Mayor Lindsay's budget, which is not enough to sweep the streets.

The mayors didn't mention the coming military budget: $75 billion requested. But the President said the war in Laos is going well. You have to put it in "perspective," he said.

It is understandable why so many of those trapped in the big cities are trying to escape. Yet, reading the findings of a survey of the nation's agricultural industry conducted in five states during the summer of 1970 by the American Friends' Service Committee, one might well ask: "What is there to escape to?"

Children, many no older than six, were discovered by the Quaker survey teams "stooping and crawling ten hours a day in 100-degree temperature harvesting crops." The committee estimated that 25 percent of the agricultural labor forces were under legal age, many working in "sweat shop" conditions, playing truant from school. "It should be intolerable for a sizable segment of a major industry to depend on child labor. In America it is not only tolerated. It is encouraged."

The survey covered states whose names conjure up visions of pastoral bliss—Maine, California, Oregon, Ohio and Washington. Out of 229 children studied in California, 19 percent were under twelve. Seventeen percent worked more than eight hours a day.

Thirty-five percent of the potato crop in one Maine county was harvested by children. A typical family of seven brothers and sisters, aged ten to sixteen, worked from 6 A.M. to 5 P.M. In the Willamette Valley of Oregon schoolteachers recruited pupils between the ages of eight and fifteen.

A high percentage of the children working lived with their families in shacks without toilet facilities or running water. Some fields had outside privies, some did not. Rarely were there facilities for washing. In all five states there are laws specifically barring child labor.

When one looks at what is being done about another urgent priority, pollution (here at least is a problem on which everyone agrees action must be taken), there are reasons for serious misgivings. In 1969, when he set up his Council on Environmental Quality, President Nixon issued a stirring proclamation: "The 1970s absolutely must be the years when America pays its debts to the past by reclaiming the purity of its air, its waters and our living enviroment." The new council would provide machinery to ensure that the coming decade "will be known as the time when the country regained a productive harmony between man and nature."

One could rest easy on *that* score—until February 12, 1971, when the nation's news media featured two stories out of Washington. First, at the White House the previous day Mr. Nixon had assured officers of more than 200 corporations, including the chief executives of several that had been recent targets of lawsuits and enforcement proceedings against pollution, that they would not be made "scapegoats" in the drive for cleaner air and water:

> The government—this Administration, I can assure you— is not here to beat industry over the head.
>
> I do not see the problem of cleaning up the environment as being one of the people versus business, of government versus business.
>
> I am not among those who believe that the United States would be just a wonderful place in which to live, if we could just get rid of all this industrial progress that has made us the richest and strongest nation in the world.

And even more disconcerting: "A Mississippi conservative with a negative voting record on conservation issues heads the House subcommittee that will deal with the funding of all federal environment and consumer protection programs," reported David E. Rosenbaum in the New York *Times.*

Representative George H. Mahon of Texas, chairman of the House Appropriations Committee, had announced the day before that he was putting these programs under the jurisdiction of his agricultural subcommittee headed by Jamie L. Whitten of Mississippi. Representative Whitten, "who has exercised enormous authority over farm programs for two decades, will thus be in control of appropriations for such agencies as the Council on Environmental Protection, the Council on Environmental Quality, the Food and Drug Commission and the Federal Trade Commission. If he uses his authority as absolutely as he has over farm legislation, he will be able to determine to a large extent how much is spent by these agencies and what the money is spent for. All air and water pollution programs, among others, will be in his domain." Here we see a politician from a Southern rural state being given tremendous power on problems that are essentially urban and industrial in nature.

Representative Whitten has never played a leading role on environmental issues, but "the League of Conservation Voters, which rates congressmen according to their votes on certain key issues, has given him a strongly negative rating." A number of leading conservationists in Congress remarked that Representative Whitten "had been skeptical of the Agriculture Department's controls on pesticides, believing the controls to be detrimental to farmers." Representative Mahon, sole authority over his subcommittee's jurisdictions, said Representative Whitten was a "real conservationist." He had been interested for a long time in "the survival of the countryside, the fading of land and the runoff of water into streams."

It is perhaps understandable why some are dubious that the 1970s will absolutely be the years "when America pays its debt to the past by reclaiming the purity of its air, its waters and our living environment." Placing the Food and Drug Administration and the Federal Trade Commission under this same subcommittee would appear to be an equally questionable decision.

Those who believe that pollution and related environmental and conservation problems represent only another tiresome sounding board for the dissidents of America to play on, a handy club with which, as Mr. Nixon put it, "to beat industry over the head," to bludgeon the political and business leaders of "the richest and strongest nation in the world," should read *On the Shred of a Cloud* by Rolf Edberg (University of Alabama Press, 1969). This thin volume, written by one of Sweden's provincial governors and most respected scientists, catalyzed under UN auspices the World Congress on the Environment scheduled to be held in Sweden during the summer of 1972. Dr. Edberg will convince all but the most ebullient that if the people inhabiting this planet are not shortly blown to bits they may well be choked and poisoned to death.

America's prominent role in the global picture can be measured by a single yardstick sentence from *The Limits of the Earth,* one of the two great works (see also *Our Plundered Planet*) written by the late Dr. Fairfield Osborn,* for many years head of the New York Zoological Society, president of the Conservation Foundation, member of the board of directors of Resources for the Future. Dr. Osborn stated: "It is difficult to absorb the thought that we Americans have used as much of the world's riches in forty years as all people, the world over, have used in four thousand! Quite a record —but can we go on like that?"

This comparison was based on the findings of an extensive nationwide study completed by the U. S. Government in the

* Both Little, Brown & Company.

early 1950s. Apropos of America's being the richest and strongest nation in the world, Dr. Osborn quotes a prominent geologist who in 1953 declared: "In fact we of the United States are now in such a position that we are not justified in hoping even to maintain our present precarious economic, political and military status quo for any considerable period of time."

And in a sentence that takes on ominous significance after nearly twenty years, Dr. Osborn warned: "The signs are about us that we have reached a turning point—the same point around which other nations, both contemporary and ancient, have revolved—some to survive, others to disappear."

It is not difficult to understand why many of the brilliant scientists, educators and other professionals who have been shunted into silence by the Nixon Administration believe today that the reassessment of "our national priorities," the transfer of "substantial amounts of funds" from "sterile war purposes to more productive ones" are of vital, urgent concern not just to the young, the old, the sick, the black, the poor but to every man, woman and child living in the land.

5

> To be a young, poor male; to be undereducated and
> without means of escape from an oppressive urban
> environment; to want what society says is available (but
> mostly to others); to see around oneself illegal and often
> violent methods being used to achieve material gain; and
> to observe others using these means with impunity—all
> this is to be burdened with an enormous set of influences
> that pull many towards crime and delinquency.
> —Report of the President's Commission on the Causes
> and Prevention of Violence, December 12, 1969

ON SEPTEMBER 20, 1971, two years after Milton Eisenhower's commission was disbanded, a week after the Attica tragedy, Lloyd N. Cutler, Washington lawyer who was executive director of the commission, declared: "I think we are going to make Belfast look like nothing in another decade."

Explaining in an interview with John Herbers of the New York *Times* that some of the members had been keeping up with developments "on an informal basis," Mr. Cutler declared:

> We feel that in the various areas of violence we covered there has been little or no abatement.

We believe there has been a substantial rise in terrorism as seen in the polarization of young blacks, in the prison up-risings and in the ambush shooting of policemen, and terror-ism is the most difficult form of violence to cope with.

During the same week of September a draft report was released by the National Urban Coalition commission set up under the leadership of Mayor Lindsay of New York and Senator Fred R. Harris of Oklahoma to evaluate conditions as they had developed since the National Advisory Com-mission on Civil Disorders (the Kerner Commission) issued its report in 1968. The draft report stated:

> Our basic finding is that, despite the Kerner report's widely accepted findings that one major cause of the ghetto rebel-lions of the 1960s was the shameful conditions of life in the cities, most of the changes in those conditions since 1968 have been for the worse.
>
> Housing is still the national scandal it was then. Schools are more tedious and turbulent. The rates of crime and un-employment and disease and heroin addiction are higher. And with few exceptions the relations between minority communi-ties and the police are just as hostile.
>
> People are angry. Perhaps they are angrier, even, than they were four years ago.
>
> The most striking point most of those we spoke with made was that they had no faith at all in "the system"—the Govern-ment and the private wielders of power—as a protector or provider. This disenchantment has plunged many into cyni-cism or apathy or despair.
>
> But in others it has inspired a new tough pride, self-confi-dence and determination.

There is a malignant aspect of American urban society for which again there is not available more than a tiny frac-tion of the money needed to tackle the concomitant gargantuan problems. A thread in the paragraph quoted above from the same final report of Dr. Eisenhower's commission —"to see around oneself illegal and often violent methods being used to achieve material gain; and to observe others using these means with impunity" leads through a murky labyrinth to organized crime generally and specifically to America's old familiar enemy and constant boon companion —the Mafia. Here it seems pertinent to ask: How can you expect a gangster-ridden nation not to spawn violence in other directions? Americans have successfully absorbed the Mafia's presence into their system and psyche, have learned to live quite comfortably with the fact that steadily rising billions of dollars are siphoned out of the national economy each year by organized crime. In spite of our law-enforcement agencies, organized crime appears to have developed into a form of *licensed* violence, condoned privately in comparison to what might be termed unlicensed violence— class violence and campus unrest.

On April 23, 1969, President Nixon sounded a call to arms when he sent a special message to Congress outlining the new Administration's plans for "waging war on organized crime and combating racketeering." The most startling fact in the message was that "illegal gambling," the prime target of the war, alone accounted for an annual "take" of somewhere between $20 billion to $50 billion, enough to finance a healthy chunk of the national defense budget. Special emphasis was to be put on an "area where we are examing the need for new laws: the infiltration of organized crime into legitimate business."

With an amount only slightly in excess of 1 percent of the national defense budget, approximately $850 million, allocated to the battle against organized crime, it seems fair to conclude that here is another "peacetime" priority that will gather dust until a less warlike atmosphere prevails. What does corrode the spirit (and the gangster presence must take its toll in cynicism and disgust from those less jaded than the middle-aged) is the vivid glimpse one gets of the festering decay resulting from the Mafia and its associates. There is space for only two examples. As is true on the political front, the news media are throwing most of the light into corners that others would prefer to keep in darkness. In "Second Business at Our Airports: Theft" (*Life,* February 12, 1971) Denny Walsh reports:

> In and around the nation's great airports, a "second business" is flourishing, one far removed from the passengers' world of plush lounges and trim stewardesses. The business is theft and labor racketeering and its target is air freight. The air freight industry is threatened by a criminal incursion unmatched since Prohibition. Cargo thieves have turned airports into a plundering ground. Mobsters and labor racketeers have infiltrated the air freight industry, forming an alliance that could soon dominate it completely. The effects of the theft and racketeering have already shown up in perceptibly higher consumer prices being charged for goods being shipped by air; eventually the price you pay for airline tickets may be affected as well.

And as for illegal traffic in narcotics, Stewart Alsop in "The Smell of Death" (*Newsweek,* February 1, 1971) states:

> New York is, in short, a city under siege. New York has at least 100,000 heroin addicts, the number is growing all the time, and these people *must* get their $40 or so a day. That means that the addicts must steal more than $1.5 billion from the people of New York every year. But that sum is a tiny fraction of the entire cost.
>
> The real cost is the death of New York as a city in which people who have any choice at all will be willing to live. Rather than live out their lives in fear, those who can afford

it are leaving the city. In time, unless the malignancy can be brought under control, New York will be a shell, its tax base wholly eroded, inhabited only by the very poor, and a tiny handful of those rich enough to insulate themselves from the surrounding sea of fear.

That gangland has a lot more money to spend than the law enforcers in New York as elsewhere was spotlighted in April 1971 when Mr. Joseph Fisch, chief counsel of the State Commission of Investigation, stated that "police corruption" is a major reason why the "war against heroin was a failure, a monumental waste of manpower and money." As "shocking examples of police corruption" disclosed by the investigation, Mr. Fisch listed "extortion, bribery, giving contradictory evidence in court to effect the release of narcotic suspects, improper association with people involved in drugs and the direct involvement of public officers in the sale of narcotics."

Because of lack of funds the United States is losing another war closely linked to crime and drugs, one that the nation simply cannot afford to lose. "The amount of research being undertaken in the United States on syphilis and gonorrhea is minuscule compared with the extent of the problem," Dr. Bruce Webster, president of the American Social Health Association and clinical professor of medicine at Cornell University, stated at an association meeting in St. Louis on April 14, 1971. Over half a million people in the United States, according to the association, suffer from undetected syphilis and are in urgent need of skilled medical attention. Each of the half million undetected victims is a "carrier" who can unwittingly spread the disease in ever-widening circles.

The same lack of money has helped create what is in some respects an equally terrifying situation on another health front. The Food and Drug Administration announced on

March 17, 1971, that the "mushrooming promotion, prescription and use of mind-affecting drugs—stimulants, sedatives, tranquilizers, and the like—are drawing critical scrutiny from the federal government and the medical profession." It was "only one of the many serious problems that confront the FDA with its limited staff and budget."

Pharmacists in 1970 filled 225 million prescriptions for mind-affecting drugs, compared to 166 million in 1965. Some psychiatrists estimate that "one-third of the adult American population has prescriptions for such mind-affecting drugs."

Dominating the contemporary American scene, towering above a cluster of lesser remaining problems which will also be solved only when "sterile war purposes" make way for "more productive ones," looms the gigantic dilemma of the educational system. So much has been written and said on the subject that one's spirits sag at the very mention of the word "education." Yet it is likely that Americans of the future will pay the most crippling penalties for what is happening—or, more appropriately, not happening—in this critical area. There is one key point on which practically everyone, of all shades of economic and political opinion, are agreed. Ranging through the entire system, in terms of both facilities and teachers, from primary and secondary schools in decaying big cities and dilapidated rural communities to thousands of universities and colleges, including the two with the largest endowments—Harvard with a billion dollars and Yale with half a billion—the root problem is money.

Overshadowing the educational system is a danger which has grown out of the lack of sufficient funds to do what has to be done. It was the only danger besides the military-industrial complex mentioned by President Eisenhower, and it was picked up by Senator Fulbright.

EISENHOWER: "The prospect of domination of the nation's scholars by Federal employment, project allocations and the power of money is ever present, and is gravely to be regarded."

FULBRIGHT: "Universities, which might have formed effective counter-weight by insistence on traditional values, have lent their power and influence to the monolith by welcoming contracts and consultantships from the military establishment, at the price of the surrender of independence, the neglect of teaching, and the distortion of scholarship."

Whether or not the American people are ready to face up to it, they must shortly answer the crucial question: Who is going to run the nation's educational system—the Government and the military-industrial complex, or the educators?

There is not much time left. Given the swiftening trend of events, if the public hesitates much longer, the question may be answered for them.

As for the over-all "peace" objectives that are not being accomplished because of "war" expenditures, it is hard to see how things can get much worse without being hopeless.

6

We see the hope of tomorrow in the youth of today.
I know America's youth. I believe in them. We can be
proud they are better educated, more committed, more
passionately driven by conscience than any generation
that has gone before.
—RICHARD M. NIXON, 1969 Inaugural Address

IF IT were not for the tragic overtones, the confrontations
between the Nixon-Agnew Administration and the youth
of America since January 1969 would be hilariously funny.
In the end the nicest boys and girls in town refused to have
anything to do with them. And the Administration in turn
dropped cold those older folks among their closest friends
who started out giving them advice on how to handle
the young.

When the International Press Institute voted Spiro Agnew
"the most serious threat to the freedom of information in
the western world in 1969," they started further: "The most
serious aspect of these attacks was that although launched
from an office which is traditionally of little effect in the
U.S. government, it appeared they may have emanated from
the White House itself."

Nowhere did this dual personality become more apparent than in the Administration's relationship with the young and their educators. Nixon and Agnew proved to be a well-rehearsed, skillful team. Sometimes the routine went so fast you could hardly tell who said what to whom. The number-two man moved into high gear shortly after Inauguration Day. A series of attacks on the young and the teachers, coupled with several barrages leveled at the news media, rose to a semi-psychotic peak in the autumn of 1969. At an October Republican fund-raising dinner in New Orleans the Vice President let go with a professionally polished out-burst that made front-page headlines and top TV billing across the nation: "A spirit of national masochism prevails, encouraged by an effete corps of impudent snobs who characterize themselves as intellectuals."

This was only a high point in an outflow of full-blown, ridiculous hyperbole that made mincemeat of another passage in Nixon's Inaugural Address:

> In these difficult years America has suffered from a fever of words; from inflated rhetoric that promises more than it can possibly deliver; from angry rhetoric that fans discontent into hatreds; from bombastic rhetoric that postures instead of persuading. We cannot learn from one another until we stop shouting at one another—until we speak quietly enough so that our words can be heard as well as our voices.

The members of the President's crime commission were very much in tune with this portion of the Inaugural Address. Their first report, issued January 5, 1969, concluded hopefully:

> Our historical and comparative analysis confirms the wisdom of Benjamin Franklin, who sagely observed upon signing the Declaration of Independence, "we must all hang together or assuredly we shall all hang separately."

Prominent in the minds of the commission members must have been one of Nixon's chief campaign promises, a promise dramatized at his Inauguration by the loudly trumpeted arrival of little Vicki Cole, a thirteen-year-old from Deshler, Ohio, who had caught the Republican candidate's eye bearing aloft a banner pleading: BRING US TOGETHER!

Little could Milton Eisenhower and his shortly-to-be-exiled group suspect that the nation was about to be deliberately hurled head first into the most bitterly divisive period in its brief history—non-intellectuals stirred up against intellectuals, hardhats against students, liberals against conservatives, blacks against whites, rich against poor, flag-wavers versus non-flag-wavers, percentages against percentages, inflamed to such a pitch many would have been delighted to hang others, including the students, rather than to hang together.

In May 1970, after the Cambodian invasion and the subsequent rise of student protest, after the fatal shootings at Jackson State and Kent State, Walter J. Hickel, Secretary of the Interior and former Governor of Alaska, in a letter to the President that was released to the news media, expressed the opinion that the Administration was "embracing a philosophy which appears to lack appropriate concern for a great mass of Americans—our young people." Hickel continued: "A vast segment of the young people of America believe they have no opportunity to communicate" with the Government "except through violent confrontation."

The letter abruptly ended this top-level relationship (the President had "personally terminated" him, Hickel explained to reporters), but the President was not diverted from the course he had charted with those whom the year before he had termed "the hope of tomorrow." On June 30, 1970, Dr. Alexander Heard, former head of Vanderbilt University, completed his term as adviser to the President on education. On July 23, in a public statement, he expressed his concern over the tide of affairs:

The President uses words that mean one thing to him but something different to many students. For example, he has emphasized that he and the students both want "peace." By "peace" students mean an end to the killing immediately. To them the President seems to mean not that but a "just peace" and "self-determination for South Vietnam."

Dr. Heard recommended that the U.S. Chief Executive should "increase his exposure to representatives of students, to university faculties and administrators, and to representatives of the Black Community and other racial minorities. He should undertake to understand the fears of 'repression' among certain groups in our country and to understand the realities underlying those fears" and "use the moral influence of his office in new ways designed to reduce tensions and help develop a climate of racial understanding."

Dr. Heard joined the former Secretary of the Interior in outer darkness. (During the last week of September 1971 he was elected chairman of the Board of Trustees of the Ford Foundation.)

Three weeks prior to Dr. Heard's retirement, on June 13, 1970, Nixon appointed a President's Commission on Campus Unrest, chairmanned by William Warren Scranton, sturdy Republican, leading candidate for the Nixon-won Presidential nomination, former U.S. Senator from and Governor of Pennsylvania, one of the prominent party members who have drifted out of the national limelight in favor of the previously unknown men who now surround the President. The commission was to investigate the general causes of campus unrest and specifically the shootings at Kent State and Jackson State.

As finally composed, the commission was made up of the

chief of police from New Haven, Connecticut; the dean of Stanford University Law School; the editor-in-chief of the *Christian Science Monitor;* the president of Howard University; a Boston College professor; a New Orleans attorney; an executive of the U.S. Department of Transportation; and a junior fellow of Harvard. It was hardly a group that could have been labeled "subversive" or "left wing." In fact, the average student might have felt it was loaded in the direction of President Nixon and the policies he was pursuing.

Yet when the commission report was issued on September 26, 1970, it was a slashing indictment of the Administration's policies. As a document it deserves a permanent place alongside others quoted above. In view of the hurly-burly rush of events since it appeared, the official reception given it and the controversy it created, one might well cogitate in retrospect for a moment on the report's highlights:

> Behind the student protests on these issues and the crises of violence to which they have contributed lies the more basic crisis of understanding. . . . A "new culture" is emerging, primarily among students. Membership is often manifested by differences in dress and life style. Most of its members have ideals and great fears. They stress the need for humanity, equality and the sacredness of life. They fear that nuclear war will make them the last generation in history. They see their elders as entrapped by materialism and competition and prisoners of outdated social forms. They believe their own country has lost its sense of human purpose. They see the Indo-China war as an onslaught by a technological giant upon the peasant people of a small, harmless and backward people.

> But among the members of this new student culture there is a growing lack of tolerance, a growing insistence that their own views must govern, an impatience with the slow procedure of liberal democracy, a growing denial of the humanity and goodwill of those who urge patience and restraint, and

particularly of those whose duty it is to enforce the law. A small number of students have turned to violence; an increasing number, not terrorists themselves, would not turn even arsonists and bombers over to the law.

At the same time many Americans have reacted to this emerging culture with an intolerance of their own. They condemn "the good as well as the bad." They resent the differences in dress and life style. If students are killed, these people feel: "It serves them right."

If this trend continues, if this crisis of understanding endures, the very survival of the nation will be threatened. A nation driven to use the weapons of war upon its youth is a nation on the edge of chaos. [Italics added.]

The commission strongly urged "public officials at all levels of government to recognize that their public statements can either heal or divide. Harsh and bitter rhetoric can set citizen against citizen, exacerbate tension and encourage violence."

The commission further urged that "peace officials be trained and equipped to deal with campus disorders firmly, justly and humanely. . . . Sending civil authorities to a college armed as if for war—armed only to kill—has brought tragedy in the past. If this practice is not changed, tragedy will come again."

The supplementary report on Jackson State concluded that the "firing by police into dormitory windows without orders and without warning" had been "completely unwarranted and unjustified." The report on Kent State strongly criticized both students and National Guards.

The commission's report was greeted in stony silence by the occupant of the White House. The national and world news media interpreted the commission's appeal to the President "to exercise his reconciling and moral leadership" and the "harsh and bitter rhetoric" comments as referring to Nixon's classic "those bums blowing up our campuses" declaration.

Three days later, on September 29, Vice President Agnew hurled himself boisterously into the breach, armed with another head-spinning message. "More Pablum for the permissivists," he declared. "The suggestion that vigorous public condemnation of anti-social conduct is somehow *ex post facto* a cause of that conduct is more of the same remorseless nonsense that we have been hearing for years."

Even the Administration's disappointment over the results of the 1970 midterm Congressional elections didn't quiet the Vice President. He was only temporarily muzzled when the Republican Governor of Oregon, during a national strategy get-together privately addressed by Agnew, told reporters he was fed up to the teeth with the VP's "rotten, bigoted little speeches."

Not until the voting age was lowered to eighteen did the nation hear its executive leader—after widely publicized, hurried conferences at Washington and San Clemente with batteries of PR advisers—come forth with two of the most astounding pronouncements in the history of American politics: The Republicans could only prosper by becoming the "party of the open door, open to all people, all races, all parties." And standing foursquare on the University of Nebraska campus: "Let us forge an alliance of the generations. Our priorities are really the same. Together we can achieve them."

President Nixon even lifted one of the late Senator Robert Kennedy's most cherished lines. He assured the youthful Nebraskans: "We can do better than this."

It took a few months to formulate all the plans for the big "youth" affair of the 1971 season. All the hand-picked, most eligible young men and women were invited—900 of them plus 500 impeccable adults. Stephen Hess, one of Nixon's

most reliable assistants, would be in charge of the cere-
monies. The Administration announced that the White
House Conference on Youth, to be held in Washington in
the early spring, would be the "most representative gathering
of young Americans ever assembled." A week before the
conference, as word got around that some of the guests, in
spite of their carefully screened credentials, might behave
boisterously, there was a change of venue to Estes Park,
tucked safely away in the Colorado Rockies.

The party was a shambles. Nothing went off as planned.
The guests showed not the slightest respect for the sponsor,
Mr. Nixon. A preamble to the resolutions adopted by the
combined 1,400 young and old conferees, which was greeted
"with standing applause by a majority of the delegates,"
read:

> Out of the rage of love for the implemented principles we
> here assert, we challenge the Government and power struc-
> tures to respond swiftly, actively and constructively to our
> proposals. We are motivated not by hatred but by disappoint-
> ment over and love for the unfulfilled potential of this nation.

Those at the conference expressed themselves in vigorous terms as diametrically opposed to the Nixon-Agnew
philosophy, words and actions. They called, among other
things, for the immediate end of the Vietnam war, the
resignation of J. Edgar Hoover, the abolition of the de-
tention-camp provision of the Internal Security Act, and
full statehood for the District of Columbia. At the final
session a photograph of Mr. Hess was pasted to the speaker's
rostrum with a slogan: "Would you buy a used conference
from this man?"

What Kingman Brewster, president of Yale, described as
an "eerie tranquillity" still hangs over the campuses of America. But one thing is certain. Many minds are busily at work
on the problem of how to persuade as many people as possi-

ble—young and old alike—that deep down underneath, in spite of everything, Richard Nixon and Spiro Agnew really and truly do think the young people of America are "better educated, more committed, more passionately driven by conscience than any generation that has gone before."

Not more than one or two misguided bums in the whole gosh-darned, wonderful barrel!

7

Ill fares the land to hastening ills a prey,
Where wealth accumulates and men decay.
—OLIVER GOLDSMITH, "The Deserted Village"

GIVEN a set of conditions such as those that have flourished in the United States during the past twenty-five years, with lush profits from armaments piling up on one side and huge portions of the population neglected on the other, there is a strong likelihood that moral and philosophical decay will set in. It has been true at intervals in the American past. It happened time and again through the centuries—in Greece and Rome, Renaissance Italy, monarchial France, Czarist Russia and, as noted by Goldsmith, in the tumultuous heyday of eighteenth-century Britain.

During such periods there is a tendency on the part of those in power to mask their intentions and their actions behind a façade of fine words, characterized by exhortations to those in more humble stations to hold true to the lofty standards of the past. Goldsmith's noble-minded contemporary, Samuel Johnson, expressed his disgust at certain aspects of life around him with a definition of *patriotism* that has become a classic. At a meeting of The Club on December

7, 1775, presided over by Charles Fox with Joshua Reynolds and the historian Gibbon among the group, Johnson proclaimed in majestic, measured tones: "Patriotism is the last refuge of a scoundrel." Recording this in his monumental life of Johnson, James Boswell explains that his mentor was referring not to those who truly love their country but to those who use patriotism as a "cloak of self-interest."

During the Christmas holidays of 1970 an English writer and archaeologist, Miss Elizabeth Callow, described to me her reactions to six years' working in New England colleges. She was full of enormous enthusiasm for the young people of America. She had found them openminded, inquisitive, friendly, of great personal integrity. One thing did worry her about quite a number of them—the philosophy expressed in such terms as "everybody else is getting theirs. Believe me when I get out I'm going to get mine too." She was afraid that the ideals of many would yield to future practicalities.

It is a pity one cannot gauge the effects on the young of some of the stories involving corruption, graft, questionable decisions, unethical practices, tax irregularities, shady real-estate and stock-market deals that crowd the TV and radio waves as well as the nation's magazines and newspapers.

In a farewell address delivered at the White House on December 21, 1970, to Mr. Nixon and a group of his intimates by retiring Presidential adviser Daniel Moynihan, there was one passage which must have bewildered a large number of young Americans, as well as a few of their elders:

> As the President has said, we are now in the middle of the journey. Where it will end we do not know. It is no longer even clear where it began, our senses having long since been dulled by the relentless excess of stimulus which is the lot of any who involve themselves in American government.

The speech was widely circulated to the overseas press through U.S. diplomatic channels as an example of the caliber of thinking going on in administrative circles. What is fascinating—apart from the admission that the group assembled didn't seem to know where they were coming from or going to—is that Dr. Moynihan didn't stop to speculate as to how the "relentless excess of stimulus" might be affecting those who were being asked to go out and risk losing their lives in Indochina—not to mention the broad mass of the American *governed,* those who can only guess from day to day what new, unexpected bombshell is about to explode in their faces.

Out of a welter of sordid tales involving less prominent public figures, three headline news stories in 1971 featuring top-level executive appointments cannot be overlooked if one is to appreciate fully the sort of political climate in which the "hope of tomorrow" is today being nurtured.

During the first week of February, when the confirmation of John Bowden Connally, former Texas Governor and Secretary of the Navy, by the Senate Finance Committee to the post of Secretary of the Treasury seemed imminent, the New York *Times* broke with a front-page story headlined: "FOUNDATION PAID CONNALLY $225,000 WHILE GOVERNOR." At the request of Mr. Connally the Finance Committee was assembled the next day by its chairman, Senator Russell Long of Louisiana. Mr. Connally gave his side of the story. The nomination by President Nixon of this prominent Democrat was confirmed by a vote of 13 to 0. Reaction in the nation's news media varied from indignation and condemnation to support for Mr. Connally. Here are the bare facts in the case.

While Governor of Texas, Connally had been quoted in his home-state press as denying that he had performed any outside services or received any outside compensation during his tenure of office.

Connally admitted he had received while Governor not $225,000 but $575,000 for services rendered before his election as a co-executor of the estate of Sid Richardson, the late oil billionaire. He explained this was "delayed compensation" spread out over a period of years for tax purposes.

The Texas state constitution forbids a Governor to receive outside compensation while in office.

Connally testified before the committee that he had learned only upon reading Richardson's will in 1959 that he had been appointed a co-executor. "Since the tax laws require the estate returns to be filed within fifteen months after date of death, we labored night and day, seven days a week, to get the estate wound up as soon as we could." In December 1960 he was offered the post of Secretary of the Navy. "So in the early part of January 1961, anticipating that I would accept the appointment . . . I agreed to set a maximum on the fees that I was to receive from the estate, and that figure was $750,000, provided it could be paid over a number of years, obviously for tax purposes." Connally became Governor in 1962, and $575,000 was paid to him between then and 1968 when he retired from office.

The key question of whether or not he had denied, to the *Texas Observer* of Austin, having received any money from the Sid Richardson Foundation while in office was, as *Newsweek* put it, "ignored." Instead of answering the question, Connally came out with a puzzling non sequitur: "The last thing I would do before this committee or any other responsible body in the government is, very frankly, to vouch for what appears in the *Texas Observer*."

Robert E. Baskin, chief of the Dallas *Morning News* Washington bureau, summed up the apathy prevailing at least in Texas if not in the nation's capital toward the ethical standards involved: "Hell, everybody in the Texas press knew Connally was receiving his fee as Sid Richardson's executor on a deferred-payment basis so the tax payment wouldn't be so hard."

What the Texas legislators who passed the law forbidding

the payment of outside monies to an incumbent Governor thought about the episode was not recorded.

William J. Casey, President Nixon's nominated candidate for the chairmanship of the Securities and Exchange Commission, was originally reported in the nation's news media as withdrawing in early February after Senate disclosures of a court case where he was successfully sued for company malpractice. Casey had paid out $8,000 for breach of the Securities Act of 1933, which requires registration of all stocks sold to the public.

In 1962 Casey had been charged by Roland H. Boggs in New York with violating the Securities Act by helping to sell Boggs $10,000 of unregistered stock in a company called Advancement Devices Inc. Casey, the sole defendant, first denied control of the company, then admitted he was chairman and had advanced $100,000 to ADI to help raise a $50,000 loan. Eventually Casey paid Boggs $8,000 in an out-of-court settlement.

Mr. Casey told the Senate committee he hadn't mentioned the case to President Nixon. A New York lawyer, he declared: "I'd forgotten about it. I don't think it is relevant." He also forgot or neglected to mention another case in 1959 when he had been named defendant in a $175,000 breach-of-contract suit. After losing a special verdict in the New York Federal Court, Mr. Casey and an associated publisher had paid out approximately $15,000 in settlement.

Despite stiff Senatorial opposition, Mr. Casey's nomination as chairman of the Securities and Exchange Commission was eventually confirmed.

During the week of August 15, 1971, in a burgeoning scandal that looked as though it might rival the most notorious happenings of the 1920s, Will R. Wilson, assistant to Attorney General John Mitchell and head of the Justice

Department's criminal division, admitted before the Securities and Exchange Commission that he had taken loans from institutions controlled by Frank W. Sharp, the millionaire Texas banker/realtor who played a key role in the development of Houston.

Wilson admitted to a $30,000 unsecured loan in August 1970, a half year before Sharp was accused by the SEC of taking money from banks and insurance companies under his control. In 1964 Wilson had borrowed $50,000, bought five acres of land, then used the land as security to borrow another $50,000. Some time later he had borrowed another $167,000—a grand total of $297,000.

Sharp, after pleading guilty to two minor charges—making a false entry in a bank ledger and selling unregistered stock—had been granted immunity by the Justice Department from further prosecution in return for aiding a grand-jury investigation into his affairs. Wilson denied helping to secure the immunity from his own department or advising Sharp what steps to take.

Sharp has been accused of giving politicians shares in his companies, then manipulating prices to afford them large profits. In the most sensational case revealed to date he had lent Texas Governor Preston Smith and chairman of the Texas state democratic committee Elmer Baum shares in one company, taking the shares as collateral on the loan. He then used his buying powers for the Houston Jesuit Fathers to buy these shares far above the market price, an operation which cost the Jesuits $6 million and made a rich profit for Smith and Baum.*

Thus one finds the Secretary of the Treasury, the head of the Securities and Exchange Commission, the Assistant Attorney General of the United States, the Governor of Texas and the Texas state democratic chairman all involved in what at best might be termed "questionable" practices.

---

*Mr. Wilson resigned on October 15, 1971.

The American public seems to be developing an immunity to shock. These sensational disclosures have caused hardly a ripple compared to the indignation felt a half century ago over more or less comparable revelations. Yet one pauses to ask: On such fare are heroes bred? In December 1970 the Yale alumni magazine ran a provocative article by Sheward Hagerty—"The Hero—He was honest, decent and true blue; In 1970, is he a square? Who was Frank Merriwell?" Like Spiro Agnew, in my boyhood I worshiped the legendary Old Eli. My bedroom walls were covered with photographs of the immortal 1923 Yale football team and those of adjacent years, a backdrop against which I must have read at least two-thirds of the 208 Merriwell books. He still occupies a special niche in my own private Hall of Fame.

And yet, after reading and rereading the Sheward Hagerty feature, one question loomed large in my mind: Who *did* kill "honest," "decent," "true blue" Frank? Certainly not the youth of today. Long before they were born Merriwell had tucked his football and baseball bat under his arm and moved off silently through the shadows to some distant Valhalla.

I found myself asking a whole series of subordinate questions having to do with his disappearance and possible demise:

Would Frank Merriwell have dropped one atom bomb on Hiroshima and then, without waiting to gauge the effect on the war-making will of the Japanese, dropped another three days later on Nagasaki?

Would he—while I was still devouring books about him —have rigged the blatant stock-market pools of the 1920s which played a key role in bringing about the Depression?

Would he have ordered the massacre of the women, children and old men at My Lai?

Or spent his time perfecting nerve gas and defoliation chemicals?

Would he have condoned in silence the flamboyant half-truths and diversive innuendos of his ardent admirer, Vice President Agnew?

Or accepted, as did Lyndon B. Johnson, the greatest mandate ever given a U.S. President on the basis of an "End the Vietnam War" promise—a plurality of more than 15 million votes—and then turn around and escalate the conflict far beyond where his defeated opponent had said *he'd* take it?

It is no surprise to me that Frank has not been seen or heard from in some time.

I suspect that when future historians sift out fact from fancy as to what has happened during the past forty years, the tarnished era I have shared with Messrs. Connally, Casey, Nixon, Agnew, Wilson, Johnson & Co., they will decide that many who are today condemned as "un-American" have fought harder to preserve the Frank Merriwell ideals than have we and our chums. Speaking for myself, I am ready to stand in line and admit that during a quarter-century of business on more than one occasion I helped do my hero in.

I also suspect many of the long-haired younger generation who have turned their backs on the mess of pottage we have handed them are unconsciously striving to create in their own image and likeness a new, brightly shining hero figure, a legendary son of a mythical Frank Merriwell, who will in his turn be "decent, honest and true blue."

On the Old Campus at Yale stands a statue in honor of Nathan Hale, the twenty-one-year-old graduate and schoolteacher who was hanged as a spy by the British during the American Revolution. As millions of American schoolboys have learned and undoubtedly still are learning, Hale immortalized himself by declaring, just before they slipped the noose around his neck: "My only regret is that I have but one life to give for my country."

It is a superb declaration, worthy of emulation. Yet in times like these it is vital for an individual, or a nation, to guard against those who would twist it into: "He who loves his country proves this solely by the sacrifices he is ready to make for it."—a sentiment expressed by Adolf Hitler in *Mein Kampf,* through which he made mugs of quite a few million of his adopted fellow countrymen. Blind obedience to authority was one despised aspect of European life in the seventeenth, eighteenth and nineteenth centuries which drove thousands to these shores. The American republic was founded on the principle that the state existed for the benefit of the individual, not the individual for the benefit of the state. Many young people would appear today to agree with our fifth President, John Quincy Adams, who, when Admiral Stephen Decatur's celebrated "My country, right or wrong," toast was repeated to him, replied: "I disclaim all patriotism incompatible with the principles of eternal justice."

Those in exalted circles who themselves appear unfit to call on others for sacrifice, or champion causes that seem unworthy to die for, should not be astonished if they foster in the young not patriotism but cynicism and distrust.

8

Coming events cast their shadows before.
—THOMAS CAMPBELL, 1777–1844

DISCUSSING the present American predicament with an old friend, I was caught off guard when he said, "The country started off rotten. Right from the start there was rampant corruption in high places. Why this longing for the good old days? It seems to me we're right in our more or less natural state."

There is of course a considerable amount of truth in what he says. The U.S. citizens of today are in some respects paying for the collective sins of the past. But there are unique factors in the current dilemma, or let's say the country has entered a far more ominous stage in a continuing, slowly intensifying drama. Up until the Civil War the faith in the early principles shared by a large majority of the people provided a powerful motivating force for the nation, in spite of many self-aggrandizing scoundrels, and this faith was shared by a fairly high percentage of those running the country. What I am opting for is a return not to the practices but to the principles of the past.

During and after the Civil War things got much worse

practicewise, but while the situation was serious it wasn't hopeless. The proof of this, as mentioned above, is that twice—during the first fifteen years of this century and again during the FDR days—the people, led by inspired men, saved the nation from disaster.

What America is faced with now is a staggering set of problems that could prove insurmountable even if there were not in power a group who on a swiftly escalating scale appear not to have any intentions of applying founding principles to the problems, who to the contrary seem headed on a narrow, self-centered course of action which by ignoring large segments of the population may in the end wreck the entire nation.

From the beginning there were some who warned against what has come to pass. As might be expected, Alexis de Tocqueville in *Democracy in America* (1835) had something most pertinent to say as to the potential dangers facing the young republic, the fledgling experiment which was looked on in his time all across the face of the earth as the hope of the world. De Tocqueville cautioned:

> The manufacturing aristocracy which is growing up under our eyes is one of the harshest which ever existed. . . . The friends of democracy should keep their eyes anxiously fixed in this direction; for if ever a permanent inequality of conditions and aristocracy again penetrate into the world, it may be predicted that this is the channel by which they will enter.

It does not tax the imagination to see the military-industrial complex against which President Eisenhower spoke in such vigorous terms as the Frankenstein progeny of de Tocqueville's manufacturing aristocracy.

De Tocqueville was not the first to warn against the emerging danger. James Madison, fourth President of the United States, half a century earlier when the Constitution was being framed, warned his fellow delegates:

In future times a great majority of the people will not only be without landed, but any other sort of property. These will either combine under the influence of their common situation; in which case, the rights of property and the public liberty will not be secure in their hands, or, which is more probable, they will become the tools of opulence and ambition; in which case there will be equal danger from another side.

Here one can translate Madison's "tools of opulence and ambition" into what Teddy Roosevelt called the "allies and instruments of the big reactionaries" more than a century later.

Alexander Hamilton, the conservative first Secretary of the Treasury, saw the need for preventing the concentration of money and power into too few hands:

Give all the power to the many and they will suppress the few. Give all the power to the few and they will suppress the many. Both, therefore, ought to have the power, that each may defend itself against the other.

Pierre Samuel Du Pont, founder of the dynasty that bears his name, would assuredly be dismayed if he could see what has happened in the last 170 years. In a letter to his close friend Thomas Jefferson, Du Pont wrote:

I bewail the fact that Americans are dragged by political circumstances into turning their capital and industries towards enterprises of the sort which do not create wealth but permit the acquisition of wealth and make it possible for a few capitalists to get hold of it.

Du Pont was one of many early American leaders in all walks of life who agreed with the thoughts of John Locke which Jefferson reshaped into the opening lines of the Declaration of Independence. In *An Essay Concerning the True, Original Extent, and End, of Civil Government,* a cornerstone of Anglo-Saxon political philosophy which the English applied partially to themselves but not to the inhabitants of their overseas possessions, Locke wrote:

> Man being, as has been said, by nature, all free, equal, and independent, no one can be put out of this estate, and subjected to the political power of another, without his own consent. The only way whereby any one divests himself of his natural liberty, and puts on the bonds of civil society, is by agreeing with other men to join and unite into a community, for their comfortable, safe, and peaceable living one amongst another, in a secure enjoyment of their properties, and a greater security against any that are not of it.

All my life I have heard, and I imagine you have too, "Ah, but all men are *not* created equal." Or "All men are created equal but some more equal than others." What Locke and Jefferson meant was that man in his *natural state as created by God* is free and equal. When he is born into an existing society not free and not equal, then that civil society is unnatural, is against nature and against the will of God. Man then has a God-given right, even a duty, to make that civil society natural. And see that it remains that way. This is not merely humanitarian; it is immensely practical. For historically time and again—most notably and recently in Nazi Germany—when rights are denied to one group or level of society, they will soon be denied to other groups or levels, including perhaps the one you yourself are in.

With the executive branch of the Government presently encroaching upon and harassing the legislative branch, it is worth taking a look at the origin point and the reason behind our celebrated system of checks and balances. Credit is usally given to Montesquieu, who in his *Spirit of Laws* wrote:

> The three powers of government must be kept separate in order that liberty may be preserved. When the legislative and

executive powers are united in the same person, there can be no liberty, because apprehensions may arise lest the same monarch enact tyrannical laws, to exercise them in a tyrannical manner.

Daniel Webster, halfway between Jefferson and Lincoln on the American scene, put into words what undoubtedly then represented in Hedley Donovan's words a "working consensus" of American minds. He wrote of the Federal Government:

> I hold it to be a popular government, erected by the people; those who administer it, responsible to the people; and itself capable of being amended and modified, just as the people may choose it to be.

Which Lincoln at Gettysburg transformed into his closing resolve: "That government of the people, by the people, for the people, shall not perish from the earth."

Some of our most revered forefathers had little use for the philosophy so ardently fought for by such as Jefferson, de Tocqueville, Madison, Webster and Lincoln. The same John Adams, our second President, who believed it was the design of Providence to use America for the "illumination" and "emancipation" of all mankind wrote late in life:

> Democracy has never been and never can be so desirable as aristocracy or monarchy. . . . Remember, democracy never lasts long. It soon wastes, exhausts and murders itself. There never was a democracy that didn't commit suicide.

Illumination and emancipation were to be accomplished under the benign guidance of the few. Washington on one occasion proclaimed: "Mankind when they are left to themselves are unfit for their own government." And Roger Sherman, a patriot especially honored in his and my home state of Connecticut—the grammar school I attended in New Haven was named after him—stated: "The people should have as little to do with government as possible." It is not a declaration engraved in sandstone over the entrance to the Roger Sherman Grammar School. At least it wasn't in my childhood.

Against such opponents Jefferson fought to ensure that the Constitution would contain a number of guarantees for the average citizen. Without him there would probably have been no Bill of Rights, no first ten amendments. Writing to the Constitutional Convention from Paris, where he was serving as Minister to France, he insisted that the Constitution should provide "clearly and without the aid of sophism, for freedom of religion, freedom of the press, protection against standing armies, restrictions of monopolies, the eternal and unremitting force of the habeas corpus law, and trial by jury in all matters of fact triable by the laws of the land."

Jefferson was purposefully trying to create in America the something that Europe was not and never had been, what no state on earth had ever been. He was seeking to protect the people not against unknown dangers but the common, recognized forms of tyranny always previously used to hold them down. He pushed through those ten amendments which today for sinister and devious reasons are being persistently undermined. In view of the current situation, one takes delight in his phrase "without the aid of sophism."

In his preface to *Natural Law,* A. F. d'Entreves wrote: "What matters is the constant endeavor to place certain principles beyond discussion, by raising them to a different plane altogether."

Jefferson managed to place certain principles beyond discussion. Or so he thought. Others just as purposefully are today trying to knock them off the plane to which he raised them, to introduce into America, as George Wald has pointed out, the very evils Jefferson tried to isolate in Europe.

In the face of fiery personal hatred on the part of the upper classes matched only in later years by those opposed to Franklin D. Roosevelt and the Kennedy brothers, Jefferson won the Presidential election of 1800. While in office he was ostracized by most of the nice people because of his democratic ideas. John Adams didn't even wait to welcome him at the White House on Inauguration Day. He drove off under cover of darkness to his home in Massachusetts.

The Reverend Timothy Dwight, president of Yale College, summed up the rabid feelings of his listeners when he stood up in his pulpit one Sunday morning during the campaign and not only pronounced Jefferson an "atheist" but predicted that if elected he would "throw the Bible on a bonfire" and that "the Marseillaise would be sung in the churches." Even worse, he added: "We may see our wives and daughters the victims of legalized prostitution; soberly dishonored, speciously polluted."

In the 1804 election Jefferson carried every state except Connecticut and Delaware. His eight years in office, followed over the next four decades by such democratic chief executives as Madison, John Quincy Adams and Andrew Jackson, kept what might be termed a reasonable balance between the rich and the rest, until the impending conflict of North versus South temporarily divided the nation not on class but on sectional lines. There were other reasons besides principles which kept the country on a relatively even keel. There was no political rallying point for the manufacturing aristocracy after the Federalist party vanished during the Jefferson-Madison regimes. On the monied side of the fence the Southern landed aristocracy dominated Washington, but the growing menace of the coming industrial Caesars is made clear by a warning sounded against them in one of Lincoln's 1861 messages to Congress:

> I bid the laboring people beware of surrendering the power which they possess, and which, if surrendered, will surely be used to shut off the door of advancement for such as they, and fix new disabilities and burdens upon them until all of liberty shall be lost.

Little did Lincoln suspect that the new Republican party which he would lead to its first national victory would become the chief political opponent of the laboring classes, in essence an unbeatable monolith. Between the Civil War and the 1929 crash, only one Democratic nominee, Grover Cleveland, would reach the White House with a clear plurality. He sneaked in twice with minuscule majorities and a defeat in between. Woodrow Wilson would never have been elected in 1912 if Theodore Roosevelt and William Howard Taft hadn't split the Republican party down the middle. Wilson received 6,286,724 votes, Roosevelt 4,126,020, Taft 3,483,922—a "Republican" plurality of 1,323,218.

From the vantage point of the Civil War it is worth setting down the three generally accepted reasons why the United States evolved at such breathtaking speed from a loose confederation of frontier colonies into, as President Nixon has put it, the "richest and most powerful nation in the world":

1.) A virtually unpopulated land mass, full of untapped natural resources, became available for settlement and development.

2.) Inventions and technological improvements in the United States and elsewhere ushered in an era of scientific advancement unprecedented in the history of man.

3.) The recently arrived inhabitants of this land were motivated by a unique and untried political, social and economic philosophy embodied in the principle that all men are created free and equal. (Whether you think they are or not is beside the point. The vast majority of early Americans, as already mentioned, accepted the principle with enthusiasm and fervor akin to religious faith.)

The importance of the third reason increases when one notes that the first two were also working in man's favor during this same period in other parts of the world, notably in Canada, Australia, New Guinea, Brazil and Argentina. Yet without reason three, progress in these land masses, again virtually unpopulated and full of untapped natural resources, has been at a snail's pace compared to the United States. This subject has been discussed with a number of people of quite varied sociological backgrounds. Almost unanimously they believe that number three, what might be called the "spiritual" factor, has been the all-important one, that without it America would have been "just another country."

Where differences of opinion take place is either in the interpretation of the principle, which at times seems to become distorted out of all resemblance to its original meaning, or where some feel the principle is no longer compatible or essential to our present well-being and future progress. The question revolves around a simple, contemporary analogy: Was the fundamental principle a booster rocket that put us into orbit, without which we can now safely remain in orbit? Or was it an integral source of power, an essential propelling force, without which we will sputter down into the mediocrity that has engulfed other promising civilizations in the past that were full of initial spiritual fervor? Those who currently are placing ends above means are in the first group. Those who believe the means make up the precious ingredient that must be preserved are in the second group.

There are two paradoxes centered around the Civil War that may help clarify this. One disappeared with the defeat of the South. The other flourished with the take-over by the Northern manufacturing aristocracy. In his magnificent three-volume *Centennial History of the Civil War,* Bruce Catton etches out in graphic fashion the paradox that was contained in the very heart of antebellum Southern agrarian society. The cheap cotton produced through slave labor on plantations and shipped to the manufacturing centers of the world was a principal factor in the growth of a new mass-producing, industrial society which eventually stormed the citadel the Southern aristocrats were trying so desperately to preserve, forces so irresistible that they brought the citadel down in flaming ruins. The seeds of destruction were in large measure contained in the cheap cotton the planters had shipped out from the citadel. It was a reverse form of Trojan horse.

The second paradox lies at the heart of American society today and may well in turn prove to be fatal to that society as we know it. Traveling through the United States, de Tocqueville observed that not just the pursuit of money motivated the industrious citizens but also the "love of the constant excitement occasioned by that pursuit." During the twenty-five years between the sultry July morning in 1934 when, at seventeen dollars per week, I entered the mailroom of J. Walter Thompson Company, then as now the world's largest advertising agency, and the crisp October afternoon in 1959 when I retired, I found the "constant excitement occasioned by that pursuit" immensely satisfying. Yet even in those neophyte days the paradox was there; it had been there since the Civil War, and it becomes increasingly obvious each year.

The "market" in those days was blanketed by publications

such as *The Saturday Evening Post, Collier's, Good House-keeping, Ladies' Home Journal.* One was regularly subjected to presentations proving that "We reach 80% of the 5% of the population who buy 90% of consumer goods," etc., etc. Network radio was reaching out into new fields, but America was still a "Woman's Home Companion" kind of cozy society, and no agency head or manufacturing executive of standing really wanted to change it. It was a Rotary Club, Kiwanis, Chamber of Commerce closed shop.

No one ever stopped to think that you could cram only so much coffee, jellied desserts, canned vegetables and margarine down one throat, could shovel only just so many bushels of breakfast food into one kiddy's tummy, could bathe one body with soap only so many times a week, could wipe the same bottom with toilet paper only a certain number of times a year. The only way they were going to get more sales was to create a situation in which more people could afford to buy the products they were giving their life's blood to push. And this was a situation they were fighting tooth and nail to avoid. They were trying to *make* money and at the same time to *keep* money, and the only way they could *keep* the money was not to give it to the people who could help them *make* more money.

Almost universally America's dynamo-powered, talented assortment of high-priced advertising and sales executives—along with the overwhelming majority of America's business and financial community in the 1930s—centered their bitter, undying animosity on Franklin Delano Roosevelt. They hated everything he stood for. And yet it was Roosevelt who blasted open undreamed-of new consumer vistas, helping the people break through to vastly increased purchasing power. As James Reston has observed, Roosevelt was responsible for a huge segment of present-day Nixon supporters who, having been admitted to the club, aren't so sure they want anybody else to join.

Back in 1961 I picked up a morning newspaper on a visit to New York and read that my old friend and associate at J. Walter Thompson, Norman Strouse, by then head of the agency, had made a speech in which he attacked the members of the Kennedy Administration as "Neo-Fabians" who were "undermining the American economy" with their socialistic New Frontier ideas. Just as FDR and his New Deal gang did back in the 1930s. Nothing had changed. Today the rising young ad man or salesman spends five days a week in New York, Chicago or San Francisco feverishly trying to convince the entire nation it is sheer bliss to own a second car, a second house, a color TV set, fancy groceries, cases of vintage Scotch, gin and bourbon, a speed boat or a ketch, lovely outfits for wives, to spend a holiday in the Bahamas or Europe. Then he spreads his weekends and his evenings in Chappaqua, Westbury, Lake Forest or Burlingame, busily devising ways to keep the less favored out of his playtime orbit, isolated somewhere in the littered landscape or gutted-out big city the ad men have done so much to create. He is caught in the same schizophrenic, paradoxical booby trap as the hard-bitten mentors of forty years ago.

With one nimble hand he is helping to produce a limitless, classless society which, with the other heavy hand, he is trying to hold back. And he cannot hold it back without slowly committing suicide himself, without destroying the way of life he is fighting to preserve, no matter how many brick walls he throws around it. You cannot yammer away at the blacks and the dispossessed morning, night and noon, telling them what constitutes a full existence, and then expect them not to want to share in that existence, even if they have to loot and riot to get it. Those polished messages of hope and promise winging out onto the air waves contain, like cheap cotton, their own seeds of destruction. They too, in reverse, are Trojan horses.

9

The big reactionaries of the business world and their allies and instruments among politicians and newspaper editors fought to keep matters absolutely unchanged. These men demanded for themselves an immunity from governmental control which, if granted, would have been as wicked and foolish as immunity to the barons of the twelfth century. Many of them were evil men. Many others were just as good men as some of the same barons; but they were as utterly unable as any medieval castle owner to understand what the public interest really was. There have been aristocracies which have played a great and beneficent part at stages in the growth of mankind; but we had come to the stage where for our people what was needed was a real democracy; and of all forms of tyranny the least attractive and the most vulgar is the tyranny of mere wealth, the tyranny of a plutocracy.
—*The Autobiography of* THEODORE ROOSEVELT

THE PARADOX that has haunted America for the past century can be detected coming into being right after the Civil War. The take-over by the manufacturing aristocracy brought in its train enormous changes and gigantic problems far more difficult to solve than the ones prior to the war. Not that it was too apparent to those living day to day at the time in America. But Henry Adams, returning to Boston in

1868 from London with his father, Charles Francis Adams, and John Lothrop Motley—both diplomats who had spent the war years abroad—records their impressions in a memorable passage from *The Education of Henry Adams:*

> Had they been Tyrian traders of the year B.C. 1000, landing from a galley fresh from Gibraltar, they could hardly have been stranger on the shore of a world, so changed from what it had been ten years before.

Against a background of self-sacrifice and devotion to duty on both sides of the Mason and Dixon Line, profiteering, opportunism, greed and graft had taken the toll exacted during any period of war—the Civil War, World War I, World War II, the war in Indochina. In *New England: Indian Summer* (E. P. Dutton), Van Wyck Brooks enlarges on the theme of the disillusionment that deadened the spirits of the Adams family and those who had shared with them the dream that America was going to be different from anything that had gone before:

> [Henry Adams] had never supposed that America would dispense with its best-trained statesmen and cast its lot for politicians who took their orders from bankers. That statesmen could be obsolete, this was a conception the Adams could scarcely comprehend; for without a thought for themselves, for three generations, they had sacrificed personal interests and local interests to the welfare of the country as a whole. They had really believed in the cause of advancing mankind, and for three generations the family had fought for the country against the British and the bankers—Downing Street, Wall Street, State Street—and triumphed in most of their struggles; and Charles Francis Adams, as Minister to England, had foiled the British again and kept them out of the war. He had raised to its highest pitch the prestige of American policy; but the bankers had prevailed in his absence. They had won the

war for the North and demanded their pound of flesh, if they had to kill the country to obtain it. John Quincy Adams, who had formed the faith of his sons and grandsons, had had a noble vision of the country's future. He had hoped to develop the national wealth on a collective, not a competitive basis. He thought there was a volume of energy stored within the Union, enough for the prosperity of all: if this could be brought into use in accordance with the laws of science, it would lead the population to perfection. For this reason, John Quincy Adams had promoted the study of science, while he fought with all his might against the bankers, who stood for competition and disruption. And now it appeared that science itself, applied in machinery and railroads, had stimulated nothing but ambition and greed.

Six years before his return to America, in 1862, Henry Adams had written to his brother, Charles, in Boston: "It will depend on the generation to which you and I belong, whether the country is to be brought back to its true course and the New England element is to carry the victory, or whether we are to be carried on from war to war and debt to debt and one military leader after another, till we lose all our landmarks and go ahead like France with a mere blind necessity to get on, without a reason or a principle."

When he went, after his return to America, to the nation's capital to offer his services, Henry Adams found himself surrounded by a new breed of political and business leaders whose aims and objectives were completely alien to his own. He described his reactions, speaking of himself in the third person, in *The Education of Henry Adams:*

> Every hope or thought which had brought Adams to Washington proved to be absurd. No one wanted him; no one wanted any of his friends in reform; the blackmailer alone was the normal product of politics as of business. . . . Grant avowed from the first a policy of drift; and a policy of drift

attracts only barnacles. . . . Grant had no objects, wanted no help, wished for no champions.

Henry Adams was not alone in his fears and doubts as to what was happening. Thomas G. Appleton in *Windfalls,* writing of the "legal" swindling that was rampant, suggested that "a gallows conveniently placed at either end of Wall Street might be useful." Charles and Henry Adams jointly in *Chapters on Erie,* an indictment of "Caesarism in business," warned that "Vanderbilt is but the precursor of a class of men who will wield under the State a power created by the State, but too great for its control." Coming events were casting long, dark shadows before.

Disillusionment was not confined to the educated thoughtful. Young men in the Union Army had been paid eleven dollars a month as privates during the first year of the war. This was later raised to thirteen dollars and then to sixteen, but, due to depreciation, the actual purchasing power of their pay was less when the war ended than when it began. These young men came marching home triumphantly to find, following a pattern that has endured ever since, that while they had been fighting, others had amassed fortunes.

No facet of American history has been more fully documented than the corruption after the Civil War. The stench of graft hung over Washington. Avarice and deceit permeated the capital, seeping out through the business and money marts of the nation. Scandal enveloped the White House, pulling into the spotlight such prominent figures as A. R. Corbin, Grant's brother-in-law, who, conniving with Jim Fisk and Jay Gould, played the key liaison role in the notorious "Black Friday" attempt to corner the U.S. gold supply, putting half the firms in Wall Street out of business; Schuyler Colfax, Vice President of the United States, who, after the New York *Sun* printed a number of incriminating letters, went before a Senate subcommittee and brazenly denied, until confronted with a canceled check, that he had participated in the loot from the Credit Mobilier swindle which netted its promoters $23 million, stuffing the pockets of scores of prominent politicians with free stock shares, catching up in its net the future President of the United States, James A. Garfield; Colonel Babcock, Grant's private secretary, whose participation in the "Whiskey Ring" scandal left a trail leading into the President's office; W. W. Belknap, Secretary of War, who resigned after being caught with his pretty wife in the bribery of post traders on Indian reservations. Grant throughout stood by his friends, with a steady stream of "I deeply regret," "I personally have full confidence in your integrity" statements flowing from the White House.

For the first time the politicians worked for the business and financial leaders who had become the real bosses of America. Never did wealth accumulate or men decay so rapidly, and no period in our history illustrates more clearly that unless the people have someone guarding their interests they will be taken inevitably to the cleaners. There is a disconcerting similarity to what is happening today—a rash of sordid cases, the legislative branch and the news media dragging the truth into the open, a shouldering aside of America's most gifted and best-trained talents. Grant turned down John Lothrop Motley as Secretary of State because he "wore a single eye glass and parted his hair in the middle."

It is hardly surprising, with what was going on in high places, that the youthful republic, still less than 100 years old, halfway home from its second centennial, was shaken to its foundations in the autumn of 1873 by a cataclysmic panic. A few economists predicted it was coming. No one paid any attention. It started with the same abruptness as the 1929 crash. On September 18 the rock-solid banking house of Jay Cooke & Company in Philadelphia abruptly declared itself bankrupt. Overextended in the financing of the Northern Pacific Railroad, Cooke & Company found itself unable to meet current obligations. Jay Cooke himself had no idea it was going to happen. The Philadelphia *Press* the next day declared: "An hour before its doors were closed, the Bank of England was not more trusted. The disaster was as unexpected as an earthquake is today."

The Cooke failure started off a devastating chain reaction. Eighty-nine railroads collapsed into receivership. The construction of new mileage halted, with some half million workers thrown out of jobs. Almost half of the 700 iron and steel plants in the country folded. Heavy borrowing from abroad had gone on for some years, and with exports falling off America was deeply in debt to Europe, a situation that didn't reverse itself until World War I. In 1873, 5,183 U.S. commercial houses failed. In 1874, the figure rose to 5,830; in 1875, 7,740. In 1876 and 1877, it went over 9,000 per annum and hit 10,478 in 1878.

For the first time in American history the principles on which the United States had been founded came under vicious attack. The manufacturing aristocracy, supported by its "allies and instruments"—in spite of having brought on the panic themselves—were determined that labor would take the rap. Although there were a few who still maintained, like Lincoln, that "labor is the superior of capital and deserves much the higher consideration," they were snowed under by an avalanche of vindictiveness. One man spoke out just as the panic started. His voice was scarcely heard, yet he sounded a timeless note of warning, as worth listening to right now as a century ago. Speaking before the graduating class of the University of Wisconsin in June 1873, the Chief Justice of that state, Edward G. Ryan, one of the ablest jurists and public figures in the Middle West, declared:

> There is looming up a new and dark power. I cannot dwell upon the signs and shocking omens of its advent. The accumulation of individual wealth seems to be greater than it ever has been since the downfall of the Roman Empire. The enter-

prises of the country are aggregating vast corporate combinations of unexampled capital, boldly marching not for economic conquests only but for political power. For the first time really in our history, money is taking the field as an organized power. The question will arise, and arise in your day, though perhaps not fully in mine: "Which shall rule—wealth or man? Which shall lead—money or intellect? Who shall fill public stations—educated and patriotic free men, or the feudal slaves of corporate capital?"

Far more popular with the monied folks during the 1870s and 1880s were the flamboyant pronouncements of the Reverend Henry Ward Beecher, the highest paid pulpiteer in the United States. Beecher, like his contemporary, D. L. Moody, was a vulgarian, a crass materialist who emphasized Walt Whitman's sorrowful comment: "Genuine belief seems to have left us." At Beecher's Plymouth Church in Brooklyn it was impossible to find a seat on a Sunday morning, so great was the crush around the sandaled feet of this eloquent darling of the profiteers and the grafters. He was a splendid example of the perennial prominent clergymen whose sensitivity to criticism of public immorality in high places is in inverse ratio to their horror of private immorality in low places, who speak of "cesspools" while dwelling in decay. His flashy, sycophantic rhetoric set a fast pace for those who are still bustling and bumbling along in his wake. The New York *Times* thus front-paged his sermon of July 29, 1877, when the country was torn by railroad strikes:

Is the great working class oppressed? Yes, undoubtedly it is. God has intended the great to be great and the little to be little. The trade union, originated under the European system, destroys liberty. I do not say that a dollar a day is enough to support a workingman, but it is enough to support a man! Not enough to support a man and five children if a man would insist in smoking and drinking beer. But the man who cannot live on bread and water is not fit to live.

The last sentence caused such an uproar among the working class that Beecher quieted down for a time. But a year later he hit another high at a convention of Union Army veterans when he declared that labor unions were one of the "worst despotisms ever bred by the human mind," adding that the "army and the great generals have proved themselves to be safer guides than the civic leaders."

The struggle for the control of the American mind and spirit was under way. The day the first Republican President had warned against had dawned, with the weight of money and power pushing hard against the "door of advancement." And for the first time the underlying democratic principles of freedom and equality were being perverted into some dark form of "European" subversion, of "Marxism" and "socialism."

In those days the hard-pressed dispossessed were not confined to the urban areas. The farmers had been knocked flat on their backs, debilitated by exorbitant shipping rates. As early as 1869, with wheat selling in the East at seventy-six cents a bushel, the railroads were charging fifty-two cents a bushel to ship it to market, leaving the farmer twenty-four cents to raise, harvest and get it to the railroads. In some cases they were also charged for grain-elevator storage. Things got worse with the passing years. By 1873 membership in the Patrons of Husbandry, commonly known as Grangers, numbered 1,600,000. The Western states started passing laws attempting to regulate shipping rates, to which the manufacturing aristocracy raised loud cries that "the foundations of property were being undermined." They branded the Grangers "enemies of law and order" (here we go, lads!) and, using a newly coined, popular catch phrase, labeled them "dangerous cranks." By 1890 farm mortgages amounted to the then staggering sum of $1,086,000, with only 10 percent of farms in some countries not mortgaged. During the next four years mortgages were foreclosed on 11,000 Kansas farms. A Government survey of fifteen Kansas counties in 1895 revealed that 85 percent of all farms were owned by loan companies.

Violence on the working-class front, mostly centered around the railroad strikes, rivaled in intensity anything that has happened during the past ten years, but in this instance it was the predecessors of today's hardhats who were on the receiving end. In 1877 the state militia fired on strikers at Cumberland, Maryland, killing ten of them. All hell broke loose, with thousands of unemployed joining the ranks of the railroad workers. Baltimore, after savage fighting, was completely taken over for several days. Thirteen men were killed in Reading, Pennsylvania, gunned down in the streets. The Pennsylvania Railroad yards in Pittsburgh were captured, shops and hundreds of loaded freight cars burned, the local militia going over to the side of the strikers and unemployed. Militia sent from Philadelphia were forced to retreat into a roundhouse but killed twenty-six of their opponents. On July 23 Chicago was taken over until federal troops arrived.

Once the strikes were temporarily settled, the owners, instead of trying to remove the causes of unrest, got tougher. Military forces were strengthened at strategic points. Better equipped, stronger arsenals were built. Secret Service agents infiltrated the unions. In 1895 General William T. Sherman of "March to the Sea" fame, head of the U.S. Army, proclaimed:

> There will soon come an armed contest between Capital and Labor. They will oppose each other not with words and arguments and ballots, but with shot and shell, gunpowder and cannon. The better classes are tired of the insane howlings of the lower strata, and they mean to stop them.

The Chicago *Tribune* commented editorially: "Hand grenades should be thrown among those who are striving to obtain higher wages."

It was against this seething background that the first "making of a President" campaign in the modern sense was held. In 1896 the power and money stood solidly behind the Republican candidate, William McKinley, while the farmers and workers, having jettisoned Cleveland for what they felt was his sell-out to Wall Street and big business, were sure they had found their champion in the youthful William Jennings Bryan. His "Cross of Gold" speech at the Democratic convention not only stampeded the delegates but swept like a prairie fire across the country. Thirty-five years later James Truslow Adams recalled: "I have never known another such wave of emotion catching up whole communities, not even our entry into the Great War or Armistice Day."

As every schoolboy knows, Mark Hanna, the Ohio millionaire, was the mastermind of the McKinley campaign. What few learn is that the Republican Presidential candidate was under heavy financial obligations to his manager. He could hardly be described as a free agent. Hanna did well by him. He pulled together the largest campaign fund in U.S. history, millions of dollars compared to several hundred thousand for the Democrats. Hanna whipped the upper classes into a frenzy of fear as to what would happen if Bryan was elected. The entire membership of the New York Stock Exchange marched up Broadway shoulder to shoulder, shouting their support for McKinley. But the big propaganda guns were aimed at the millions of workers.

Goethe once observed that the two greatest enemies of mankind are hope and fear. The Republicans pulled out all the stops on both primary emotions. Their slogan was "A Full Dinner Pail," but they didn't count on hope alone. The Saturday before Election Day hundreds of thousands of laborers received slips in their pay envelopes telling them that if Bryan was elected they needn't come back to work the next day; the factory would be closed. During the course of the campaign Bryan was publicly branded a "traitor," a "madman" and an "anarchist." The vitriol continued to flow even after the election. The New York *Tribune* stated:

> He goes down with the cause and must abide with it in the history of infamy. He had less provocation than Benedict Arnold, less intellectual force than Aaron Burr, less manliness and courage than Jefferson Davis. He was the rival of them all in deliberate wickedness and treason to the Republic.

A highly revealing glimpse of the Republican campaign strategy is afforded by a letter Mrs. Henry Cabot Lodge, wife of the U.S. Senator from Massachusetts, wrote shortly after the election to Sir Cecil Arthur Spring-Rice, who later became the British Ambassador to the United States. Stating that the Republicans had spent $7 million to Bryan's $300,000, Mrs. Lodge combined exultation at victory with uninhibited admiration of Bryan's personal magnetism and the uphill battle he had waged:

> The great fight is won. It was a fight conducted by trained and experienced and organized forces, with both hands full of money, with the full power of the press—and of prestige —on one side; on the other, a disorganized mob at first, out of which burst into sight, hearing, and force—one man, but such a man!
>
> Alone, penniless, without backing, without money, with scarce a paper, without speakers, that man fought such a fight that even those in the East can call him a Crusader, an inspired fanatic—a prophet! It has been marvelous. Hampered by such a following, such a platform—and even the men whose names were our greatest weapon against him deserted him and left him to fight alone—he almost won. We had during the last week of the campaign 18,000 speakers on the

stump. He alone spoke for his party, but speeches which spoke to the intelligence and hearts of the people, and with a capital P. It is over now, but the vote is seven millions to six millions and a half.

Even Whitelaw Reid, publisher of the New York *Herald,* grandfather of the present New York member of the U.S. House of Representatives, allowed personally and begrudgingly that perhaps Bryan wasn't quite as bad as Benedict Arnold, Aaron Burr or Jefferson Davis. Said Mr. Reid: "When a man polls as many votes as he has received for the Presidency, I suppose there must be something in him."

At the start of the twentieth century it appeared as though a "permanent inequality of conditions and aristocracy" had indeed once again penetrated into the world. In 1904 a nationwide study revealed a mimimum of 5,300 independent manufacturing plants swallowed up by 318 trusts with a combined capital of $7,246,000,000. How many small businessmen had been ruined in the process was not revealed.

The previous year the *Wall Street Journal* stated that the amount of power flowing into the hands of a small group of influential bankers was "not merely a normal growth but concentration that comes from combination, consolidation, and other methods employed to secure monopolistic power. Not only this but the concentration has not been along the lines of commercial banking. The great banks of concentration are in close alliance with financial interests intimately connected with promotion of immense enterprises, many of them being largely speculative." The control of banking power, continued the *Journal,* was centering more and more in those who were primarily interested in "stock promotion, watering and manipulation."

Other studies showed that the J. P. Morgan and John D. Rockefeller groups, the two principal aggrandizing complexes, held between them 314 directorships in 112 banks, railroads, insurance companies and miscellaneous corporations with a combined total of $22,245,000,000 in assets. In an after-dinner speech one tycoon remarked that it had been said that the business of America was controlled by twelve men and that he was one of the twelve. True enough, he agreed, after which his publicity henchmen spent several frantic hours keeping the statement out of the newspapers.

Some idea of how wealth was accumulating is furnished by the amounts various individuals left behind them. When Cornelius Vanderbilt died in 1877 he was worth $105 million. When his son died eight years later the amount had spiraled to $200 million. In 1848 the first Astor in America, described by the New York *Herald* as a "self-invented money-making machine," had set a record with a residue of $20 million. Forty-two years later the son of the third John Jacob Astor inherited $100 million from his father. But these figures swiftly faded into insignificance. Before 1912 John D. Rockefeller had become America's first billionaire. In the early 1920s Henry Ford would take pleasure turning down a check of $1 billion as a proposed purchase price for the Ford Motor Company. Just before the 1929 crash Andrew Mellon, the third member of the exclusive club, had with his immediate family not capital amounting to $100 million but an annual income estimated at more than $97 million.

In 1931, looking back at the early 1900s, James Truslow Adams observed in *The Epic of America*:

> The comparatively simple social and governmental problems of 1787 had become so overwhelmingly complex that it is a question today whether we or any other nation are going to be able to solve them by intelligence or whether we shall become the victims of uncontrolled forces.

In 1911 the wealthy New York clubman Frederick Townsend Martin was lambasted by his fellow socialites as a "traitor to his class" when his book *The Passing of the Idle Rich* stated in no mincing fashion what he thought the activated rich were doing to America:

> It matters not one iota what political party is in power or what President holds the reins of office. We are not politicians or public thinkers; we are the rich; we own America; we got it, God knows how, but we intend to keep it if we can by throwing all the tremendous weight of our support, our influence, our money, our political connections, our purchased senators, our hungry congressmen, our public-speaking demagogues into the scale against any legislature, any political platform, any presidential campaign that threatens the integrity of our estate.

Americans at the turn of the century had a chance to flex their muscles in a war—not much of a war: a warm-up, comic opera fracas in which we punched Spain in the nose. It gave the propagandists a chance to try out a few slogans. There were some who noisily proclaimed that America was about to assume her worldwide Manifest Destiny, but no one took them too seriously. We intervened in Cuba originally because some $50 million in U.S. investments were threatened when the natives rose up against their Spanish overlords, but at least we still admired the underdog enough to go in on the side of the Cubans.

There was one political figure at the time who would have felt right at home today, who if he were still on the scene would surely be a fair-haired favorite of the military-industrial complex. U.S. Senator John Mellen Thurston of Nebraska trumpeted from the floor: "War with Spain would increase the business and earnings of every American railroad, it would increase the output of every American factory, it would stimulate every branch of industry and commerce."

When President McKinley was assassinated in 1901 and Vice President Theodore Roosevelt, former Governor of New York, succeeded him in the White House, few could have suspected from his conservative background and rough-riding antics during the Cuban embroilment that the new President would have an abrupt and profound influence on the course of American political affairs. It is immensely refreshing to see how much the right man in the right place can accomplish, even in a system as complex as our own. No one was more stunned than the vested interests by what the first Roosevelt did when he assumed office. They had regarded him as "their" man. It is not overstating the case to say that Teddy Roosevelt, through having a conscience of his own, one comparable to Gladstone's in his later years, helped the American people to rediscover their own collective national conscience. Comparing what happened then to what is happening today, William V. Shannon concluded in the New York *Times* on September 15, 1971:

> At every level of government and in almost every corner of our common life, there is need for a regeneration of public morality and a rededication to social justice such as swept the nation in the progressive era during the first decade and a half of this century.

By now it should be clear that no extreme measures are being advocated in these pages to help cure America's ills. The dispossessed, the aged, the young, the blacks should not have to resort to protest and violence to get what they deserve as American citizens. This is a plea to average men and women to wake up to what is happening to their own rights and heritage, to realize that only by extending the franchise in the true sense of the word and by diverting the national course from war to peace will they themselves be able to continue or, rather, to resume the enjoyment of life, liberty and the pursuit of happiness.

There is one key statement by Theodore Roosevelt that should be framed, rushed over to the White House and placed in front of the Presidential desk:

I am following out the Jackson-Lincoln theory of the Presidency. Namely, that occasionally great national crises arise which call for immediate and vigorous executive action, and that in such cases it is the duty of the President to act upon the theory that he is the steward of the people.

Richard Nixon is fond of saying that Theodore Roosevelt is one of his chief philosophical inspirations. Compare the above with his "strict construction of the Constitution," his partisan, diversive, percentages-against-percentages tactics which have convinced many he would rather be President than right, that his silent acquiesence not only condones but encourages his Vice President in the constant flouting of democratic principles, a calculated process that would have been anathema to Theodore Roosevelt.

We ourselves might take to heart a passage that appears in James Truslow Adams' *The Epic of America*:

I have little trust in the wise paternalism of politicians or the infinite wisdom of business leaders. We can look neither to the government nor to the heads of the great corporations to guide us into the paths of a satisfying and humane existence as a great nation unless we, as multitudinous individuals, develop some greatness in our own individual souls. Until countless men and women have decided in their own hearts, through experience and perhaps disillusion, what is a genuinely satisfying life, a "good life" in the old Greek sense, we need look to neither business nor political leaders.

Theodore Roosevelt had several underlying factors working in the direction of the course he had charted for the United States. Hundreds of thousands of Americans were beginning to devote a considerable amount of leisure to reading. Meticulously documented, thoroughly researched, scarifying studies of what had been going on in the U.S. political and economic arenas for 125 years had become available. Some of them led to direct legislative action to curb the abuses they exposed. Ida Tarbell's monumental *History of the Standard Oil Company* (1904) was the single most important reason why the trust was broken up by the U.S. Supreme Court in 1912. Upton Sinclair's best seller *The Jungle,* in 1906, despite vicious opposition from lobbyists and legislatures, led to wide-scale reforms in the Chicago meat-packing industry. (See George Horace Latimer's *Letters from a Self-made Merchant to His Son* for the lobbyists' answer to Upton Sinclair's facts.) J. H. Bridge, W. A. Croffut, S. C. T. Dodd, Thomas W. Lawson, Henry Demarest Lloyd, Gustavus Meyer, G. H. Montague were others who helped remove the blinders from the eyes of the American public.

Overwhelming in its impact on public opinion was the straightforward, objective way the nation's press reported the United Mine Workers strike in 1902–1903. As labor battled for recognition during the last years of the nineteenth century, the violence had become increasingly bitter, the attempts to hold down the working class ever more brutal. In 1892, during the Carnegie Steel strike at Homestead, Pennsylvania, 300 Pinkerton detectives hired to guard the plant shot ten strikers dead, wounded another sixty. General Sherman's prediction, made in 1895, of an "armed contest" between capital and labor was in fact already a bloodstained reality. It took 8,000 National Guardsmen to crush the "revolt."

In 1893 federal troops were ordered in to break the back of the miners' strike in the Coeur d'Alene district of Idaho. In 1894, over the unavailing protests of Illinois Governor Stephen Altgeld, Grover Cleveland sent federal troops to Chicago to put a messy "shot and shell" end to the Pullman strike. The Haymarket bombing in 1896, for which four men, in spite of wide differences of opinion as to their guilt, were hanged (Governor Altgeld brought more righteous wrath down on his head when he pardoned three of the convicted strikers), and other turbulent episodes saw the politicians and business leaders, the clergy, other opinion leaders and the vast majority of newspapers lined up in a sturdy phalanx on the side of law and order. For the first time, during the United Mine Workers strike, the reading public was given a day-by-day, week-to-week, blow-by-blow description of actual conditions in the Pennsylvania coal-mining regions. Clarence Darrow presented the evidence. The national press reported it accurately. And Theodore Roosevelt, unlike any President since Abraham Lincoln, took a stand shoulder to shoulder with the workers.

More than anything else the strikers were helped by the incredible statements of the mine owners and operators. Their chief spokesman, George F. Baer, president of the Reading Railroad, the Philadelphia and Reading Coal and Iron Company and several lesser operations, as a warm-up let go with:

> The rights and interests of the laboring man will be protected and cared for, not by the labor agitators, but by the Christian men to whom God in His infinite wisdom has given the control of the property interests of this country.

Baer placed himself in arrogant opposition to the President of the United States. In a patronizing declamation he stated:

> The duty of the hour is not to waste time with the fomenters of this anarchy and insolent defiers of the law, but to do what was done in the war of the Rebellion, restore the majesty of law and reestablish order and peace at any cost. The government is a contemptible failure if it can only protect the lives and property and secure the comfort of the people by compromising with the violators of law and the instigators of violence and crime.

"Contemptible failure" was not to be passed over unnoticed by Teddy Roosevelt.

These were two of what Irving Stone in *Clarence Darrow for the Defense* describes as "four immortal phrases minted by George Baer, four phrases which were to do more to bring about industrial democracy in America than the heroic flailing of Darrow and his fellow liberals." The other two warrant repetition:

> We refuse to submit to arbitration before the Civic Federation, because they are to decide not whether the wages paid are fair, but whether they are sufficient to enable the miners to live, maintain and educate their families in a manner comformable to established American standards and consistent with American citizenship. More impractical suggestion was never formed. It would require many years of examination to determine just what those standards are and to determine whether it meant that a man should earn enough money to send his son to Yale or Harvard or to some modest college like Franklin and Marshall, where we keep down expenses.

And as Darrow brought into the open the plight of the miners and their families, many of whom had been imported to the United States "for the very reason they were accustomed to poverty, because they could subsist on the smallest possible quantities of food under the direst living conditions, because they could be worked hard for small wages, Baer cried out in protest: 'They don't suffer! Why, they can't even speak English!'"

Summoned to the White House for a conference which was a complete flop, Baer announced to the press that the operators objected "to being called here to meet a criminal, even by the President of the United States." Roosevelt said later: "If it wasn't for the high office I hold I would have taken him by the seat of the breeches and the nape of the neck and chucked him out of that window." Only when the

President threatened to take over the mines by force and operate them did the owners agree to a commission of arbitration. It was a symbolic victory. The average weekly pay was raised from $10.09 to $11.09. A nine-hour working day was established. The UMW union wasn't recognized. But with the help of the U.S. Chief Executive a precedent had been established.

Theodore Roosevelt, besides reversing the stance taken on capital and labor by every President since the Civil War, was also the first to take vigorous steps to try to stop the mounting concentration of wealth in a few hands by way of trusts and other pyramiding combines. In 1890 Congress, as a sop to public opinion, had passed the Sherman Anti-Trust Act, but out of the initial eight prosecutions there had been only one conviction. During the entire five years McKinley held office, with trusts mushrooming in every direction, not a single indictment was brought. In 1895 an attempt was made to break up the Sugar Trust, but, although American Sugar Refining and its associated companies controlled 98 percent of total volume, the Supreme Court ruled that a "monopoly of manufacture was not a monopoly of commerce." This stupefying decision was reversed during TR's Administration.

The President singled out as his first primary trust-busting objective the Northern Securities Company. This holding corporation, set up as a compromise by the Morgan–James Hill and Harriman rival groups with a combined capital of $400 million, controlled the Northern Pacific, the Great Northern and the Burlington railroads—the first two of which were parallel lines. When J. P. Morgan heard that the Government was about to file suit he said he was disappointed. He had thought "Mr. Roosevelt would do the gentlemanly thing." In 1904 the company was dissolved by the Supreme Court, a success which led to other convictions and dissolutions.

In terms of his own favorite football vernacular—in this small particular he and Nixon bear a slight resemblance to each other—Roosevelt got the ball moving in the right direction, and, in the face of widespread abuses and fierce opposition, it continued to head that way up until the start of World War I. In 1903 Roosevelt set up a Department of Commerce and Labor whose original intent was to protect the economic interest of the public. From 1900 until his retirement in 1909, 219 million acres of forest land were removed from public sale. During the last few weeks before leaving office, riding down savage legislative opposition and intensive lobbying activities, he pushed through a National Conservation Commission. Two measures which the Republicans had always fought until his Presidency—a graduated income tax and the election of U.S. Senators by popular vote—came into being in the 16th and 17th Amendments, which were subsequently ratified during the Taft Administration. The Sherman Act was amended by the stronger Clayton Anti-Trust Act under Wilson. The Federal Trade Commission was established about the same time. In a gallant effort to control the "money trust," a Federal Reserve Banking System also came into being in 1913, but in 1929 it failed in its objective. Over-all tariffs were reduced from 37 percent to 27 percent. The theme of a "New Freedom" sounded in Wilson's 1913 Inaugural Address must have struck a warmly responsive note in the hearts of a sizable "working consensus" of Americans—Republicans and Democrats alike:

> The great Government we loved has too often been made use of for private and selfish purposes, and those who used it had forgotten the people. At last a vision has been vouchsafed to us of our life as a whole. We see the bad with the good, the debased and the decadent with the sound and vital. . . . There has been something crude and heartless and

unfeeling in our haste to succeed and be great. Our thought has been, "let every man look out for himself, let every generation look out for itself," while we reared giant machinery which made it impossible that any but those who stood at the levers of control should have a chance to look out for themselves. . . . We have come now to the sobering second thought. . . . We have made up our minds to square every process of our national life again with the standard we so proudly set up at the beginning and have always carried in our hearts. . . . We shall restore not destroy. We shall deal with our economic system as it is and as it may be modified, not as it might be if we had a clean sheet to write upon. . . . And yet it will be no cool process of mere science. The Nation has been deeply stirred, stirred by a solemn passion, stirred by the knowledge of wrong, of ideals lost, of government too often debauched and made an instrument of evil. . . . This is not a day of triumph; it is a day of dedication.

10

All of what may be perhaps described as intangible power—power of wealth, power of government, and the new power created by vast industrial combinations—has this common characteristic with what we know as tangible, or physical power. Power of all kinds, properly controlled, wisely and intelligently used, is of inestimable value to mankind and lies at the bottom of our progress in civilization. But uncontrolled, unregulated, it becomes a constant menace, a very real and perpetual danger to civilization itself.
—FRANKLIN DELANO ROOSEVELT, December 10, 1929

IN 1914 Wilson's glowing vision of the future went literally up in smoke, the smoke rising from thousands of smokestacks hurriedly erected to meet the unprecedented demand for munitions and supplies from across the Atlantic. Once again avarice and dishonesty ran riot, although even a dim picture of what really happened didn't emerge until the Congressional investigation of the 1930s.

In the first month of the war Charles M. Schwab, president of Bethlehem Steel, brought back from England the largest single order for munitions ever secured by any country in history. During the same month Du Pont got an order for 100 million pounds of gunpowder at about double the peacetime rate. From 1914 to 1916 our annual overseas shipments of explosives rose from $6 million to $467 million. In their best prewar year Du Pont's gross sales had amounted to only $36 million. Total dividends for the war period amounted to four times the par value of the stock. With overseas orders for explosives skyrocketing every month, the U.S. Government decided to build a smokeless powder plant of its own. Du Pont, asked to help in its construction, reluctantly agreed, but in return for giving away trade secrets proposed a deal through which they would have netted $43.5 million. They finally settled for $2 million. Pierre Du Pont, testifying before a 1934 Congressional committee, admitted that Newton D. Baker, Wilson's Secretary of War, had told him he considered the Du Ponts a "species of outlaws."

A new profitable field of endeavor—war—had been discovered. Peacetime had never been like this. The material rewards started to pour in rapidly. By July 1916 nearly $1.3 billion worth of U.S. securities owned abroad had found their way home, principally from Britain. By the end of the war, from having started as a debtor nation owing *$3 billion* overseas we became a creditor nation owed *$10 billion*. That was the magic wave of the wand which overnight made us the "richest, most powerful nation in the world." There had never been such an abrupt turnaround in man's history. Yet ten years later, thanks to the manipulators and the speculators, we were right back on Skid Row, flat on our collective asses.

As to what World War I cost the taxpayers: The Treasury paid out $22 billion up to the Armistice, plus $9.5 billion lent to our allies that was never repaid. By the end of 1936, with bonuses, pensions, etc., the Treasury estimated total cost, direct and indirect, at $36 billion. Nothing illustrates more graphically how much the United States changed during those four fateful years than the fact that this $36 billion, for *war* expenditures only, compares to a total figure for *all* Government expenditures, including five wars, of less than $25 billion during the 124-year period from the first National Congress to Wilson's inauguration in 1913. This same $36 billion amounts to about half of our current annual defense budget. Although during the First World War the few were rapidly gobbling up millions in war profits and spiraling stock-market prices, in the end the many got nothing. Abe Martin, the homespun contemporary humorist, summed up how ordinary citizens fared when he remarked, "All we got out of the war was out!"

Once America declared war, opportunities for worldly advancement, if you knew which strings to pull, became limitless. The War Department was characteristically lavish and careless in its expenditures. Although there were only 86,-000 horses in the services, 1 million horse covers were ordered by "gold-plating" purchasing officers. Not to mention 945,000 saddles, 2 million feed bags, 2 million halters. For a maximum of 4 million soldiers, 35 million pairs of heavy hobnailed boots were bought. Twenty-five million pairs were left at the end of the war which were disposed of at prices less than the price of shoelaces. Twenty million mosquito nets were also bought by the Army, but not one was ever shipped overseas.

Nobody has ever been able to figure out how much the Mellons made out of the four aluminum gadgets which were standard equipment for all enlisted soldiers. Stewart H. Holbrook, who served as a doughboy in the trenches, refers to them in his informative *The Age of the Moguls* as "impedimenta." They consisted of

> one aluminum mess kit, one aluminum canteen and holder used for a cup, one aluminum bacon can, and one aluminum condiment can. [The canteen and cup and the mess kit were] light, serviceable and of use. The other two items, which belonged to a day when soldiers carried and cooked their own

rations, were absolutely worthless. They were worse than that; they were added burden and they took up space. But we lugged these two worthless things over much of Europe. They had to be displayed on our bunks for daily inspection. We cursed them daily. We cursed the men who thought them up. We cursed the men who made them. . . .

Enormous profit, however, lay in supplying us with this needless stuff—impedimenta of the worst kind. We had not then heard of the Mellons, but most of us did know of something called the Aluminum Trust and we bellyached about it with the typical fervor of the set-upon enlisted man. I still recall the shock, delayed until about 1919, of learning that fortunes could be and were made during wartime.

Due largely to a decision handed down by William Howard Taft while a federal judge in Cleveland, Ohio, the Mellons had obtained an unbreakable monopoly on the manufacturing and sale of all aluminum products in America. (In time they secured a monopoly on bauxite, the basic ore from which aluminum is refined.) After Andrew Mellon, the largest single contributor to Warren Harding's campaign fund, became Secretary of the Treasury in 1920, one of the most "constructive" measures he pushed through "to protect the American working man" was a 250 percent duty on all foreign-produced aluminum.

Holbrook sketches out in vivid highlights other complicated Mellon manuevers through which they gained control of the Gulf Oil Company and the Koppers Company. Andrew was so little known in 1920 that, according to Harry Daugherty, Harding's Attorney General, when he was suggested for a Cabinet post, Harding replied: "Mellon? I don't know him." The Pittsburgh billionaire was described as looking like "a tired, double-entry bookkeeper afraid of losing his job; worn, and tired, tired, tired." Having reduced taxes on higher incomes as much as 40 percent and secured tax refunds of over a million dollars each for three corporations controlled by him and his associates, Mellon announced, two months *after* the Wall Street debacle, on January 1, 1930: "I see nothing in the present situation that is either menacing or warrants pessimism. During the winter months there may be some slackness or unemployment, but hardly more than at this season each year." At which time Henry Ford, one of America's two other billionaires, was busily writing: "We now know that anything which is economically right is also morally right. There can be no conflict between good economics and good morals."

Within three years there were 15 million Americans out of work.

Among major World War I scandals were blockbusters involving shipping and shipbuilding, aircraft engines, and the Alien Property Custodian's Office. In April 1919, 4,500 German chemical and dyestuff patents were handed over by this Government agency for $250,000 to the Chemical Foundation. They were worth well over $100 million. These bargain-priced patents formed the nuclei for some of our extremely profitable drug manufacturing companies. It was under the friendly auspices of this same Alien Custodian's Office that the indefatigable Andrew Mellon got control of Dr. Heinrich Koppers' rightful 20 percent share of the Koppers Company.

Into the thick of the shipowner profiteering waded the equally indefatigable J. P. Morgan. His firm held large financial interests in the International Mercantile Marine Company and several other British shipping lines which for the first time in their history were making fantastic profits. When a bill was introduced into the House of Representatives calling for the purchase of available ships owned by neutrals and for the construction of Government-owned freighters in American shipyards—a piece of legislation loudly condemned as "rank socialism" by the hard-liners—Morgan appeared in Washington to argue against passage.

Under astute and no doubt well-rewarded leadership a marathon filibuster talked the bill to death. It took two years to get new legislation enacted, by which time the British Isles were nearly strangled to death by German submarines and the cost of ship construction had risen from $60 to $260 per ton. In his autobiography, *Crowded Years,* William Gibbs McAdoo, Wilson's Secretary of the Treasury and the "Father of the Federal Reserve System"—who was continually blasted for his spearheading support of the Shipping Bill—wrote:

> Appalling prices were paid for anything that had to do with a ship. Engines and other equipment were purchased at such staggering cost that I fancied more than once that the machinery we were buying must be made of silver instead of iron and steel.

Following the well-established formula that when the American taxpayers *buy* they pay through the nose but when they *sell* they get nothing, these silver-plated ships were sold off after the war by the Harding Administration at ridiculous figures. The Dollar Line got for $550,000 apiece five handsome vessels that cost $4,128,000 apiece to build. More than 200 ships built for $750,000 per head were sold for less than $3,000 per head. Another 100 freighters for which the public had shelled out over $250 million were knocked down for $25 million. One is acutely reminded of Senator William Proxmire's remark that "In some respects, the United States has been transformed from the arsenal of democracy into a gigantic supermarket."

Why a person who objects to such extraordinary squandering of public funds should be smeared as "unpatriotic" and "leftist" or even called "liberal" is difficult to understand,

but the process has been going on for fifty years and continues unabated. With the take-over of Russia by the Soviets in
1919, one finds a bewildering, heightening confusion in the
United States as to the differences between Marxist tenets
and democratic principles. It was a confusion of meanings,
of interpretation—an opportunity for increased perversion
—which is still with us and lies near the roots of our political
and economic dissensions. Against a background of anar-
chistic bomb scares, the Sacco-Vanzetti trial, Ku Klux Klan
depredations and a steady drop-off in labor-union membership due to what looked like an unending period of broadly
based prosperity, one could detect among the upper strata
disdain and distrust of the very word "democracy." Many of
the newly rich were more inclined to look on their wealth as
divinely inspired than were some enlightened members of
longer established families. Just as the passage from Frederick Townsend Martin's *The Passing of the Idle Rich* mir-
rors the sentiments of a considerable portion of well-to-do
Americans during the conscience-stirring reign of Teddy
Roosevelt, so the following excerpt from *Mumbo Jumbo* by
Henry Clews, Jr., published in 1923, echoes the feelings of
hundreds of less loquacious, more discreet U.S. plutocrats
during the uninhibited Harding-Coolidge-Hoover era:

> Although the word democracy is the largest, ugliest and
> most grotesquely ornate receptacle of salivary vulgarity, mawk-
> ishness and hypocrisy in the dictionary, there are compara-
> tively few men of today who would not with a cringing gesture
> of mob-servility hold it to their lips and drink deep from it in
> order to quench their thirst for popularity with the mass, which
> democrats despise in proportion to their elevation above it.
> As the moral health, entertainment and happiness of the pro-
> letariat is entirely dependent upon the moral health and hap-
> piness of a limited aristocratic governing class, it necessarily
> follows that the proletariat is at present far from being happy,

since it finds itself led by riff-raff arrivists, high priests of vul-
garity, machine powered larrikins, sentimental, pharisaic bour-
geois, overfed idealists and scientific fanatics.

When you strip away the hothouse hyperbole (what a
phrase-maker Clews would have been for our current executive crown prince!), the belief that "the moral health, enter-
tainment and happiness of the proletariat is entirely
dependent upon the moral health and happiness of a limited
aristocratic governing class" would appear to be wholeheartedly embraced by a wide spectrum of Bill Buckleys, George
Wallaces, Billy Grahams, Martha Mitchells, Curtis Le Mays
and Spiro Agnews, plus assorted generals, diplomats, politicians and businessmen, trooped after by their benighted
followers.

As one looks back on the 1920s, what strikes one most
vividly is how few people suspected what was really going on
behind the scenes. Even more, how few people had the
slightest inkling as to what was about to happen. In many
cases, including that of Andrew Mellon, they didn't understand what had happened *after* it happened. While there were
rumblings of fraud and corruption which erupted occasionally during Harding's tenure of office, on the whole people
felt they had indeed been led "back to normalcy" by their
poker-playing Chief Executive, whose comment on his own
nomination was "We drew to a pair of deuces and filled."
Certainly the prevailing climate was less disconcerting and
foreboding of trouble than the one we have lived in for the
past seven or eight years. During the "Keep Cool with
Coolidge" era and the regime of the "Great Engineer," an
overwhelming majority of Americans were blissfully convinced that never in the history of the world had a nation's
destiny been entrusted to such sage, conscientious and dedicated leadership, a view enthusiastically concurred in by the
leaders themselves.

Even today one is inclined to divide the ruling Republicans of that vintage into good guys and bad guys, yet it is fascinating to reflect on how closely they were all linked to one another from the beginning. At the apex of the pyramid stood the "Big Boob in the White House," as the President was familiarly referred to by his "Ohio Gang" chums who plotted their sordid intrigues down at the Little Green House on K Street. The best that can be said of Harding is that, like U. S. Grant, he was more sinned against than sinning.

Next on the totem pole came "Silent Cal," whose most memorable comment on national affairs was the profound observation, "When a great many people are out of work, unemployment results." Coolidge had been catapulted into the big-time by a single statement that must have been written by somebody else. During the Boston police strike, as Governor of Massachusetts he had dispatched a wire laying it right on the line that "There is no right to strike against the public safety, by anybody, anywhere, at any time." That bowled the boys over, and Coolidge vaulted into the Vice Presidency.

Among those gathered around the Cabinet table was a mixed bag, including the impeccable Charles Evans Hughes as Secretary of State, destined to be Chief Justice of the Supreme Court but still not fully recovered from Wilson's nosing him out of the Presidency in 1916; the infamous Harry Daugherty as Attorney General; the nearly bankrupt Albert F. Fall, the Secretary of the Interior who would go to jail for his part in the Teapot Dome scandal; Andrew Mellon, his pockets bulging with war profits, running the Treasury; and Herbert Hoover, who was embarking on eight platitudinous years as Secretary of Commerce. For years friends have been advising me that if Hoover had won in 1932 he would have straightened everything out in a few months, that he was already starting to do some of the wiser things Franklin D. Roosevelt did, and would have done them better without upsetting the "traditional American way of life."

Having forced myself to read practically every campaign speech and public statement attributed to him, all I can say is that if there was ever a bigger boob in the White House than Harding it was Hoover. Whereas Harding and Coolidge didn't profess to know much, Hoover was the greatest self-appointed prophet and prognosticator who ever sat in the White House, bristling with statistics and projections on subjects which, judging from what happened, he knew less about than the lowliest janitor on Capitol Hill. More than any other American public figure he should serve as an enduring monument to James Truslow Adams' advice not to put our trust in the "wise paternalism of politicians or the infinite wisdom of business leaders," for Hoover was both. Here is a smattering of the data on which my conclusions are based regarding this greatest of all proponents of unleashed American "initiative," whose cardinal sin, the one that endears him to you in spite of what he and his associates did to the country, is that he honestly believed in what he preached.

After a campaign of subtle innuendo and semi-secret vilification directed against the Democratic Presidential candidate, Governor Alfred E. Smith of New York—unmatched since the heyday of the late Quattrocento Florentines—which ended in November 1928, with Hoover capturing all but six states, including eight Southern states and the "Happy Warrior's" home state, Ray Lyman Wilbur wrote:

> The Presidential campaign of 1928 was as significant as that of 1860. Not since the Lincoln-Douglas debates has the country followed the issues of a campaign with more intensity. The speeches of Mr. Hoover were measured statements of a new liberalism facing new conditions with courage and confidence in the human individual to act wisely for himself and his neigh-

bors. They clarified the citizens' relationship to the great economic mechanism resulting from the practical application of
invention, discovery, and widespread education.

The public gulped down every ounce of this intoxicating
brew. They had been conditioned to do so. In early September 1928 Hoover had explained to a spellbound Midwest
audience that "due to the ingenuity and hard work of our
people and the sound policies in government, we have come
to be the greatest reservoir of the world's wealth." In spite
of his eight years as Secretary of Commerce during which he
hobnobbed regularly with Andrew Mellon, Hoover either
didn't realize or didn't want to let the folks know that it was
World War I itself that had turned our $3 billion world deficit
into a $10 billion credit. Nor quite obviously did he suspect
that within thirteen months we would toss the last remaining
chips on the gaming table, much of it lost in the "worthless
bonds of bankrupt nations."

In another campaign speech Hoover sent everybody home
to bed happy when he informed them:

> We in America today are nearer to the final triumph over
> poverty than ever in the history of any land. The poorhouse is
> vanishing from among us. We have not yet reached the goal,
> but given a chance to go forward with the policies of the last
> eight years, we shall soon with the help of God be in sight of
> the day when poverty will be banished from the nation.

He was given the chance to go forward. Apparently God
was the only one listening to periodic warnings from the
Federal Reserve Banking System that things were not quite
as rosy as Hoover was painting them. And in another
heart-warming campaign reassurance:

> With impressive proof on all sides of magnificent progress,
> no one can rightly deny the fundamental correctness of our eco-
> nomic system. . . . Our whole business system would break

down in a day if there was not a high sense of moral responsibility in our business world. . . . The whole practice and ethics of business has made great strides of improvement in the last quarter of a century, largely due to the effort of business and the professions themselves.

The "high sense of moral responsibility" referred to by the Republican candidate will be examined in a moment in the light of revelations during the 1930s. On October 22, 1928, exactly one year and one week before Black Thursday ushered in seven days during which the value of securities listed on the New York Stock Exchange dropped $30 billion, just as a starter, Hoover explained:

> When the war closed . . . we were challenged with a peacetime choice between the American system of rugged individualism and a European philosophy of diametrically opposed doctrines—doctrines of paternalism and state socialism. The acceptance of these ideas would have meant the undermining of the individual initiative and enterprise through which our people have grown to unparalleled greatness.

That was the date—October 22, 1928—when the phrase "rugged individualism" was born. Quite a far cry from Teddy Roosevelt's "malefactors of great wealth." Another breathless promise came into being about the same time: "Prosperity is here to stay."

There was one portion of the public to whom Mr. Hoover couldn't speak with such pride, but he did spiel off some pretty convincing double-talk that helped pile up an enormous plurality in the farming states. He promised he would apply the same sound scientific principles to agriculture that had paid off so swimmingly for business and finance. He omitted to mention that the banks had taken over through mortgage foreclosures during his first two years as Secretary of Commerce the lands of over 300,000 farmers, and that locked up in a desk drawer was a U.S. Government study made earlier that same year of 1928 which revealed that farmers who produced eighteen basic agricultural products received $7.5 billion for those products, while the consumers who bought those same products paid for them $22.5 billion. In this instance statistics would only have confused them.

On March 8, 1930, more than four months after the Stock Exchange disaster had hit America in the solar plexus, President Hoover confidently predicted that the minor setback "would be over in sixty days." This was two months subsequent to Mellon's cheery New Year's Day message re "some slackness or unemployment."

In July 1930, when a harassed delegation of business leaders arrived at the White House begging the Chief Executive to do something to relieve the situation, Hoover blithely advised them, "Gentlemen, you are six weeks too late. The crisis is over!"

In October 1930, addressing the American Bankers Association, Hoover warmly congratulated the assembled captains of finance:

> During the past year you have carried the credit system of the nation safely through a most difficult crisis. In this success you have demonstrated not alone the soundness of the credit system, but also the capacity of the bankers in an emergency.

During the next twenty months 3,000 banks with total deposits of more than $2.5 billion shut their doors, unable to pay back millions of customers who had placed their faith in the hands of Harding, Coolidge, Hoover and their cohorts. It was during this bleak period of three years, according to my "conservative" friends, that Hoover was doing so much to get the economy back into motion.

As for what was actually going on during those predepression years when the "whole practice and ethics of business" was making "great strides of improvement," Charles Anson Beard's *America in Mid-Passage* (Macmillan, 1939) describes a number of disclosures made during the U.S. Senate investigations of 1932 which should help recharge our forgetters and inform the young as to what happens when the public's interests are not properly safeguarded. To quote:

> A few examples will illustrate process too vast for a description short of the original full hearings. In 1928 the earnings of the Kolster Radio Corporation dropped in the direction of zero and the directors were disquieted; but a way of flight from ruin by unloading the wreck on the public was quickly discovered. Rudolph Spreckels, chairman of the company and chief stockholder, called in the aid of George Breen, "the hero of a hundred pools," gave him options on Kolster stock, and set him in motion. Mr. Breen thereupon engaged the interest and cupidity of a number of prominent stock brokers and hired a newspaper publicity man to prepare the people for another opportunity to "invest in America's prosperity." In a short time news of "highly favorable developments in Kolster business" was circulated among brokers and insinuated into the columns of the press. With "public interest" receptive, Mr. Breen and his brokers started "the big push"—buying and selling huge blocks of Kolster stock, all the while managing to raise the price as eager watchers rushed to share in "a good thing." In the course of this "unconscious and automatic" market operation, the price of the stock was lifted from 74 to 96, over 20 points, as the insiders gradually sold off their holdings. When they withdrew from "the killing" Kolster stock slid down to its "natural" value, reaching five or six dollars a share in December, 1929. Then in January, 1930, the bubble burst; the company went into the hands of receivers.

Out of this "smart business deal" Spreckels made over $19 million; Breen made over $1,300,000. One brokerage firm collected $182,000 in commissions, and the public got stuck. Breen stood up before the Senate committee and declared: "It was all legitimate." He hadn't manipulated, only "stabilized" the market.

On a much larger but no loftier plane was the Anaconda Copper pool:

> In this experiment in stabilization the very paragons of private and public virtue participated—John D. Ryan, Thomas E. Bragg, partner in a prominent brokerage firm, and Charles E. Mitchell, head of the National City Bank and its investment affiliate. With the aid of his institutions, his colleagues, his brokers, his high-powered selling agents throughout the country, Mr. Mitchell bought and sold Anaconda stock, churned the market, ran up prices, "stabilized" the market somewhere between 60 and 135, and sold out to "investors." Before many months passed Anaconda stock plunged downward to about four dollars a share.

The public took a beating of about $160 million on this deal. The profits of the "legitimate members of the banking and brokerage fraternities" can be imagined. Beard comments: "There seemed to be justification for Arthur M. Wickwire's phrasing: 'The Anaconda crushes its prey.' "

Beard describes another operation popular during the period when no one could deny "the fundamental correctness of our economic system," popularly known as "price pegging," holding the price of a new security up until the distributors had unloaded on the public:

> Such an operation was well illustrated by the case of the German bonds issued on June 12, 1930, through a syndicate under the leadership of J. P. Morgan & Company. The inside of this business transaction in the "automatic and unconscious" market was unfolded by the Senate Committee early in its inquiry. The witness was Richard Whitney, President of the New York Stock Exchange and head of a brokerage house—destined to an assignment in Sing Sing prison a few years later. . . .
>
> From June 12, the day of the public offering, to July 2, 1930, the syndicate operated in the market, buying and selling the German bonds and keeping the price on a level with or above

the offering price of 90. This operation Mr. Whitney's house had carried on "under order . . . through J. P. Morgan & Company." On July 2, after the syndicate had disposed of the entire issue to investors, it "pulled the plug," to apply the characterization of the Street, and let the securities take care of themselves. Almost immediately the price sagged below 90, and on the day of Mr. Whitney's explanation the German bonds were selling at 35 or 36 cents on the dollar. Mr. Whitney made it clear to the senators from the "provinces" that it was "an absolutely usual and customary method of merchandising and distributing securities."

Another custom which aroused the curiosity of the Senators was the so-called preferred list, special customers who received securities at prices under the market prices. Here are a few names from the J. P. Morgan list. It was never explained by the Morgan partners what these people did in return for the House of Morgan. The partners were in fact wondrously unaware as to exactly what these "preferred" people did in life:

CHARLES FRANCIS ADAMS	Secretary of the Navy under Hoover
NEWTON T. BAKER	Secretary of War under Wilson
BERNARD M. BARUCH	"Philosopher General" of the Democratic party
CHARLES T. HILLES	Co-Manager of the Republican party
J. R. NUTT	Former Treasurer, the Republican party
WILLIAM H. WOODIN	First Secretary of the Treasury under FDR
NORMAN H. DAVIS	"Ambassador to the World" under Hoover and FDR

WILLIAM GIBBS MC ADOO	Secretary of the Treasury under Wilson
FRANK L. POLK	Undersecretary of State under Wilson
SILAS STRAWN	Former president, the U.S. Chamber of Commerce
OWEN J. ROBERTS	Associate Justice of the U.S. Supreme Court
GENERAL JOHN J. PERSHING	Commander of the A.E.F.
WALLACE E. DONHAM	Head of the Harvard Business School
JOHN J. RASKOB	Chairman of the Democratic National Committee
JOHN W. DAVIS	Democratic candidate for President (1920)
CALVIN COOLIDGE	Former President of the United States

A neat, impartial list. The practice of keeping a friendly foot in both camps was already well established.

When one who has lived through such a wide-open era of wholesale buccaneering reads today of nominations to the U.S. Supreme Court, the SEC chairmanship, the Justice Department, the post of Secretary of the Treasury which are hotly challenged on ethical grounds, of bribery, graft and fraud cases involving numerous officials in positions of trust, it is natural to speculate as to what is really going on behind the somewhat grimy façade. Given the same kind of free-wheeling conditions, are human beings going to behave differently than in the past? It would be nice if this time we could keep the roof from caving in on our heads, thus avoiding spending the next ten years digging our way out of the debris. Or perhaps this time not being able to dig our way out.

The words spoken by Franklin D. Roosevelt quoted at the head of this chapter were spoken less than two months after Wall Street's Black Thursday. The voice of the orator would become familiar not only to most contemporary Americans but to millions of people across the face of the earth. Except possibly for Winston Churchill's, it would become familiar to more people than any other voice in history. But on December 10, 1929, Roosevelt was still Governor of New York, regarded with distrust by many of his own party's bigwigs, including some whose names appear on the J. P. Morgan "preferred" list. If it hadn't been for the rapidly worsening events unfolding around Roosevelt, Herbert Hoover no doubt would have been re-elected in 1932 and would have been succeeded by an unbroken chain of more Hardings and Coolidges. And FDR would have been remembered by only a handful of historians, close friends and members of his family.

The most remarkable thing about his December 10, 1929, speech is that in spite of all the confusion, the conflicting opinions, the blindness of those in charge of national affairs, Roosevelt already saw with unique clarity what was happening and why it had happened. Right then he charted a new course for the nation, or, more accurately, like the first Roosevelt, he steered the nation back toward its original course.

Not in that speech or in any of his written or spoken statements can one find a trace of "Marxism" or "pro-communism." There is no better example of the power of propaganda than the fact that still today millions of Americans believe Herbert Hoover was a splendid, enlightened leader, a defender of the American way of life, while Roosevelt was a sinister left-winger. FDR and Teddy Roosevelt were cousins worthy of each other. Their thoughts and actions ran along surprisingly parallel lines. FDR also focused attention on the dangers inherent in an unbridled manufacturing aristocracy, in a "tyranny of plutocracy," and his opponents screamed bloody murder because he hit them where it hurt.

If we did nothing more than follow the advice in that early landmark address, we could throw away the gas masks, the M4 rifles, the bombs and the brickbats. We would be well on our way toward rediscovering ourselves as a nation. Here are the highlights of what—at a time when others were talking about "rugged individualism" and the "sense of moral responsibility in our business world"—our thirty-sixth President had to say:

> The historian will record the last fifty years as marking more progress in the liberation of the individual from the drudgery of the daily struggle for existence than in all the centuries that have gone before. And this is true not only of our country but of other nations in the world. The human individual the world over has realized that poverty and starvation and killing manual labor are not an inevitable necessity in his life, and he has found a common voice with which to demand as today's necessities what were yesterday's luxuries. . . . Universally he demands not only life and liberty but that pursuit of happiness which our own forebears laid down as one of the fundamentals of the rights of a citizen.
>
> Before this demand that governments must subordinate the glory of the state to the welfare of the humblest citizens, the citadels of conservatism, which means leaving things alone as they are, are being swept away, and even China has torn loose from ancient traditions in this vast world movement for better things.
>
> It is a new phase of civilization. . . . It lies back of the increasing understanding that we must take care of our infirm in mind or body or estate; and in this country, it underlies some willingness to acquiesce in vast combinations of industrial enterprises because of the theory that such combinations, if, and only if, they are honestly conducted, bring within the

reach of many, things which only a few years back were the costly playthings of the rich.

Because we have discovered that vast numbers of manufacturers and combinations of manufacturers employing hundreds of thousands of men can produce things which make for our own ease at prices within our income and in so doing can produce millionaires at the top and better paid workmen at the bottom we have without much thought given our tacit approval to such combinations and have indeed become so obsessed with their apparently magical power that during the recent period of wild speculation and senseless inflation any half dozen of decrepit and moribund industries by merely pooling their individual debts and inefficiencies could attract the public money to any stock issue they chose to float because they were a combination, a merger, or a holding company.

Because they have seemed at least to bring us prosperity and to bring us comforts and luxuries, it has become unfashionable to speak even a whisper of warning against the danger of letting them eventually assume the mastery of us all. They should be good servants. Let us beware lest they become bad masters. Too much we have placed them in positions of almost unlimited power. We must see to it that they are at all times under such control of government as will prevent them from becoming Frankensteins of our own creation.

Given a vision of what might yet be, the people did not perish.

11

The American Revolution is for everybody.

—THOMAS JEFFERSON

THREE of the legendary giants of the nineteenth century—an American, a Scotsman and a Frenchman—shared in common a passionate belief that in the eyes of God every human being is equal in intrinsic value to all other human beings. Further, that to be true children of God, people must approach the problems of this world accordingly. All three regarded the principle of democracy as divinely inspired.

These three men and a host of others who shared their views kept the intellectual and spiritual flame of democracy burning throughout the period stretching from the early days of the republic into the present, playing a vital role in the shaping of the political and economic philosophy of the two Roosevelts, Woodrow Wilson, Adlai Stevenson, the Kennedy brothers and those who rallied to their banners.

Certain passages written by the three men summed up the democratic principle in terms that became world-famous. Today perhaps to some they seem old-fashioned, flowery, out of date—which could be a reflection not on the last century but on ours. Certainly what is presently happening in the United States, weighed against these passages, can only be described as tragic.

Herman Melville, in the preface to *Moby Dick,* wrote:

> Men may seem detestable as joint stock-companies and na-
> tions; knaves, fools, and murderers there may be; men may
> have mean and meager faces; but man, in the ideal, is so no-
> ble and sparkling, such a grand and glowing creature, that
> over any ignominious blemish in him all his friends should run
> to throw their costliest robes. That immaculate manliness we
> feel within ourselves, so far within us that it remains intact
> though all the outer character seems gone; bleeds with keen-
> est anguish at the undraped spectacle of a valor-ruined man.
> Nor can piety itself, at such a shameful sight, completely stifle
> her upbraidings against the permitting stars. But this august
> dignity I treat of is not the dignity of kings and robes, but that
> abounding dignity which has no robed investiture. Thou shalt
> see it shining in the arm that wields a pick or drives a stake;
> that democratic dignity which, on all hands, radiates without
> end from God; Himself! The great God absolute! The center
> and circumference of all democracy! His omnipresence, our
> divine equality.

Thomas Carlyle, in *The French Revolution,* describing the people of France as they were in the latter part of the eighteenth century, wrote:

> With the working people, again, it is not so well. Unlucky!
> For there are twenty to twenty five million of them. Whom
> however we lump together into a kind of dim compendia
> unity, monstrous but dim, far off, as the *canaille;* or more hu-
> manely, as "the masses." Masses indeed; and yet singular to
> say, if, with an effort of imagination, thou follow them over
> broad France, into their clay hovels, into their garrets and
> hutches, the masses consist all of units. Every unit of whom
> has his own heart and sorrows; stands there covered with his

own skin, and if you prick him he will bleed. What a thought: that every unit of these masses is a miraculous man, even as thyself art; struggling, with vision or with blindness, for *his* infinite Kingdom (this life which he got, once only, in the middle of Eternities); with a spark of the Divinity . . . an immortal soul in him!

Alexis de Tocqueville in the preface to *Democracy in America* expressed the view that all of us, wittingly or unwittingly, contribute to the progress of democracy. (See Irving Stone's comment that the blithering statements of George F. Baer did more to help U.S. industrial democracy than anything said or done by the liberals.) De Tocqueville wrote:

> The various occurrences of national existence have everywhere turned to the advantage of democracy; all men have aided it by their exertions: those who have intentionally labored in its cause, and those who have served it unwittingly; those who have fought for it and those who have declared themselves its opponents, have all been driven along in the same track, have all labored to one end, some ignorantly and some unwillingly; all have been blind instruments in the hands of God.

Unless you share Carlyle's belief that "every unit of these masses is a miraculous man, even as thou art," then the intense excitement of participating in philosophical democracy has passed you by. And there can be no hedging. No qualifications as to color. Or race. Or religion. Either you believe it or you don't believe it. No "We will bomb them back into the Stone Age." No 4 percent. Or 51 percent. Or 98 percent. *Every* unit. One hundred percent. Lieutenant William Calley and every old man, woman and child in the ditch. Whose skin bled when it was pricked.

Searching through history from the earliest records, even in the realm of myth and legend, one finds faint traces of the working of the democratic principle, from the beginning through to John Locke and Thomas Jefferson, glimpses of the doctrine that the essential element in society is the worth and significance of the "single" individual, not the power and glory of the "collective" state.

Many scholars single out as the first person to expound the principle Ikhnaton, ruler of Egypt in the fourteenth century before Christ. Ikhnaton preached the revolutionary doctrine that there was "only one god and he dwelt universally in the hearts of all men." It was revolutionary on two counts— monotheism and universality.

Eight hundred years later, in India, Mahivra, better known as Jina, the founder of Jainism, taught this same essential doctrine. Mahivra attacked the entire caste system, preaching that "All men, low-caste and high-caste, are equals." Yet after his death he was deified, eventually becoming the focal point for a highly intricate pantheism in which the gods themselves were divided into castes.

Forty years after the birth of Mahivra a son was born to a wealthy rajah in the Ganges River valley. His true name, Siddhara Gautama, is almost forgotten today, for it is he who is remembered as Buddha, the "enlightened one." Like a number of other religious leaders, he gave up a luxurious life while still in his twenties and he too spoke out against the caste system· "A man does not become a brahmin by his family or birth. In whom there is truth and righteousness— he is blessed, he is a brahmin."

Gautama created a monumental revolution in thought built around the simple principle of equality. Until his time in India only the rich and the powerful were thought worthy of salvation. Five hundred years later, when Asoka, Emperor of India in 264 B.C., embraced Buddhism and spread it throughout the Far East, the democratic principle was all but submerged beneath a complicated structure of ritual and priesthood, of costly temples and expensive sacrifices. There is a striking parallel between the relationship of Buddha to Asoka and of Jesus to Constantine I, who legalized Christianity and apparently embraced it himself four centuries after Christ. Gautama and Jesus would have understood each other. Asoka and Constantine would have understood each other. Any cross-dialogue would undoubtedly have required lengthy interpretation.

The two most influential philosophers in Chinese history also preached the "glorious doctrine." Lao-Tze, born in 604 B.C., lamented the "poverty of the poor" and, surveying the scenes of carnage and inequality around him, cried out against the "great disorder." He advised: "The wise man doth not accumulate. The more he expends for others, the more doth he possess of his own, the more he giveth to others, the more hath he for himself." Lao-Tze was utterly opposed to pomp and circumstance, war and class, wealth and ostentatious worship. Yet, following the inevitable pattern, the essence of his teachings was buried under a slag heap of temples, priests, idols and sacrifices—the religion of Taoism. Today on a lofty mountain peak in Kiang-si Province lives a high priest who calls himself and is called by millions T'ien-shi, the "Heaven Master."

It is difficult to think of Lao-Tze—or of Buddha—without thinking of St. Francis and the sleepy sun-drenched town of Assisi. There is a parallel symbolism. This twenty-six-year-old young man, also the son of a wealthy merchant, inspired by Christ's message, "get you no gold, nor silver, nor brass in your purses," in 1208 appeared with his long-haired, untidy hippie friends on the terrace of the papal palace in Rome among the satin-gowned dignitaries and persuaded Pope Innocent III to allow him to set up an Order of Poverty. In 1226 he was buried at his own request among the paupers and lepers in an unmarked grave outside the walls of Assisi; now, 750 years later, one goes back to find the ornate, richly panoplied, double-tiered cathedral rising above where they believe his bones must lie.

Kung-Fu-Tze, better known as Confucius, born in 551

B.C., after a brilliant career as a scholar and minister for justice in Chung-tu Province became a wanderer among the people. "With whom should I make fellowship," he asked, "save with suffering mankind?" "To give oneself earnestly to the service of men, and while respecting the spirits, to make no great to-do about them—that is wisdom."

In both classical Greece and Rome one finds excellent examples of the booster-rocket analogy. Greece, moved by legends of individual greatness stemming back to Prometheus, who stole fire from the gods to give to mankind, soared to unmatched pinnacles culturally and philosophically within the framework of the first historic limited democracy, amassed material wealth, developed into an oligarchy and within several centuries committed suicide in a vicious downward spiral of city-state against city-state, class against class within each city-state. The disastrous effects of the Peloponnesian War ruined Athens; the short dictatorship of Sparta was succeeded by the Macedonian and Roman conquests.

In one of the most penetrating studies of nationalist power ever written, Thomas Callander, late professor of Greek at Queen's University, Ontario, in *The Athenian Empire and the British* (Weidenfeld and Nicolson, London, 1961)—a volume that should be required reading for all aspiring to political leadership in the United States—reversed himself after a near lifetime as a hard-line Tory and built a devastating case that "greed and envy" were the fatal elements in both the Greek and British empires:

> The beggarly profits that, in the antique world, dazzled the war party and conducted their dupes to the quarries of Syracuse, were but a drop in the bucket compared with the gold of the Rand, priorities in world markets, privileges, concessions, oil wells and countless raw materials whose monopoly fomented jealousy and worse in the past one hundred years.

Callander, basing his conclusions on Plato's two related beliefs that "all wars are fought for gain" and that the "rampant vice" of his early era was the false doctrine "Justice is the interest of the stronger," sums up his own profound reflections:

> No amount of superiority, physical, mental or moral entitles the stronger community to coerce the weaker and no recital of natural or acquired advantages or excellences by the aggressor improves his case.

President Nixon's "America is the richest and most powerful nation in the world" is worth tossing up beside some of the prattlings of the nineteenth-century imperialists quoted by Callander, especially in view of the shattered ruins of the British Empire that stretch like Ozymandian reminders today around the surface of the globe.

LORD ROSEBERY:
> How marvelous it [the British Empire] all is! Built not by saints and angels, but the work of men's hands; cemented with men's honest blood and a world of tears, welded by the best brains of centuries past; not without the taint and reproach incidental to all human work, but constructed on the whole with pure and simple purpose. . . . Do we not hail in this, less the energy and fortune of a race than the supreme direction of the Almighty?

CECIL RHODES:
> We happen to be the best people in the world, with the highest ideals of decency and justice and liberty and peace, and the more of the world we inhabit the better it is for humanity. . . . We, the English-speaking people, have the power to gather the whole civilized world into one great Empire; every inch of it that is fit for white habitation. What about the whole continent of South America, the sea-board of China and Japan, the Holy Land, Mesopotamia, the Malay Archipelago? It's

our duty to build up this irresistible power. When once this is done, war, man's greatest misfortune, will be impossible. However, you and I had better begin with Africa.

JOHN RUSKIN:

This is what England must do or perish. She must found colonies as fast and far as she is able, formed of the most energetic and worthiest of men; seizing any piece of fruitful land she can set her foot on and there teaching her colonists that their chief virtue is fidelity to their country and that their first aim is to be to advance the power of England by land and sea.

Bang! Crash! Slam!

Today we are inclined to remember the "grandeur that was Rome" and forget that it was four centuries of a Roman *republic* that supplied the motivating booster force, the democratic principle so deeply cherished by a broadly based, generous-minded citizenry, epitomized in the hour of peril by such as Cicero, the Scipios, Brutus, which propelled the Roman *Empire* on through five centuries of festering and internal decline and decay. Though the challenge of Julius Caesar was successfully met, the methods employed by Augustus, first and most brilliant of Rome's emperors, provide a case history of how one ruthlessly ambitious politician, supported by equally ruthless henchmen, can artfully swindle a whole people out of their hard-won rights, "to fix new disabilities and hardships upon them until all of liberty shall be lost"—without more than a handful suspecting what was happening, so skillfully and with such slick propaganda was it done. Augustus, perhaps more than any person in history, brings home the significance of Gustave Le Bon's observation that "The art of those who govern consists above all in the science of employing words."

In the dawning of Christianity—the blending together of the best of Judaism with the best of Platonism, brought together more through Philo of Alexandria than anyone else—one can detect the democratic principle, not so much as a political but as a philosophical or religious concept, reverberating throughout the whole known world as never before and never again until the Renaissance. And never before or since has such a condemnation of the evils of power and wealth misused been sounded as with the advent of Christ upon earth.

Thomas H. Huxley, Darwin's mightiest champion, his mind and eyes searching with objective, scientific clarity, saw the political significance when he wrote:

> The Bible has been the Magna Carta of the poor and the oppressed; down to modern times no State has had a constitution in which the interests of the people are so largely taken into account, in which the duties, so much more than the privileges of rulers, are insisted upon.

It is impossible to find anywhere a more emphatic and colorful condemnation of plutocracy, of the "tyranny of mere wealth," and along with it a passionate belief in the kinship of all mankind as when the voices of Jesus and His disciples rang out across the land. It is almost embarrassing to call oneself a *Christ*ian in the light of what he said:

> "It is as easy for a camel to pass through the eye of a needle as for a rich man to enter the Kingdom of Heaven."
>
> "What profiteth a man if he gains the world and loses his soul."
>
> "The stranger that dwelleth with you shall be as one born among you and thou shalt love him as thyself."

One hundred headlines from the past ten years leap to mind. Referring to the rich: "Between us and you there is a great gulf fixed."

Christ chose the following verse from Elijah to read to the Galileans:

The spirit of the Lord is upon me, because he hath anointed me to preach glad tidings to the poor; he hath sent me to heal the broken-hearted, to preach deliverance to captives, and recovery of sight to the blind, to set the down-trodden free.

And attacking the pillars of the community:

They put heavy loads of the Law upon men's shoulders but they won't lift a finger to help them. They wear wide scripture texts and large tassels. They like the best seats at dinners and the front seats in the synagogues but they are hypocrites, blind fools. They let the weightier matters of the Law go—justice, integrity, and mercy.

There is a disconcerting sameness about the past and the present.

You clean the outside of the cup and dish but inside they are full of greed and self-indulgence. You are whited sepulchres. Outwardly you appear to be upright but within you are full of hypocrisy and wickedness. How can you escape being led to the pit? The publicans and the harlots will go into the Kingdom of Heaven before you.

Subversive stuff! Stronger than anything quoted from the two Roosevelts, Dwight and Milton Eisenhower, Abraham Lincoln, Thomas Jefferson, James Truslow Adams, Pierre Samuel Du Pont, de Tocqueville, Thomas Carlyle, Herman Melville and others. No wonder they crucified Him before they deified Him.

Nothing is more terrifying to contemplate than the fact that the "civilized" world, having achieved during a thousand years philosophical, artistic and cultural goals in many respects loftier than what has been accomplished during the past five hundred years, slid back or was shoved back into a thousand years of repressive authority. It was a millennium during which, except for isolated pockets of scholars, the knowledge and wisdom of classical times not only faded from the memory of man but in many instances was deliberately obliterated by those in control of worldly and spiritual matters. In the face of inquisitorial rigidity on questions of dogma and doctrine, of brute force used to hold down political liberalism, of ceaseless persecution of those who tried to give a more scientific or rational explanation of the workings of the physical world, one can yet detect the stirrings of the Renaissance, the shadows of coming events—although here "shadows" is hardly the appropriate word—as early as the twelfth century. Again, despite the popular concept of the Renaissance being dominated by princes and ecclesiastical potentates, in the beginning it was the importance of the individual that launched mankind once more into orbit.

Walter Pater in *The Renaissance* appropriately states the case:

> This outbreak of the human spirit may be traced far into the middle age itself, with its motives clearly pronounced, the care for physical beauty, the worship of the body, the breaking down of those limits which the religious system of the middle age imposed on the heart and the imagination. . . .
>
> The Renaissance of the fifteenth century was, in many things, great rather by what it designed than by what it achieved. Much which it aspired to do, and did but imperfectly mistakenly, was accomplished in what it called the *eclaircissement* of the eighteenth century, or in our own generation; and what really belongs to the revival of the fifteenth century is but the leading instinct, the curiosity, the initiatory idea. . . .
>
> The essence of humanism is that belief that nothing which has ever interested living men and women can wholly lose its vitality—no language they have spoken, nor oracle beside which they have hushed their voices, no dream which has

once been entertained by actual human minds, nothing about which they have ever been passionate, or expended time and zeal.

It is this "essence of humanism"—the universality of interest in all mankind—that is woefully lacking in official U.S. circles today. Except for the Kennedy New Frontier days it has been lacking for some time. Instead we find the self-centered failing that prompted President Truman to refer to the Russians as "those Asiatics," that causes the present White House incumbent to preen himself because we are the "richest and most powerful nation in the world," that brings forth "stone age," "little brown brothers," "they can't even speak English" anti-humanist declarations.

The three hundred years that separated Petrarch, the "Father of the Renaissance," from John Locke and Thomas Jefferson witnessed an outpouring of human creativity and original thought that rivaled the classical period and outweighed anything that has come since. It is not overstating the case to say that the establishment of the American republic represented the only attempt to put into action the philosophical essence of the Renaissance. That is why so much hangs in the balance. What will the American experiment prove to be? Triumph or tragedy? Will it succumb to the propagandists and their blandishments, to old lies dressed up in new raiment? Or will the concept of government by, of and for the people not perish from the earth?

There is only room to mention a handful of the many who shaped the course of man's destiny from the fifteenth to the eighteenth century, each of whom contributed in his own way to the creation of the American republic.

Shakespeare: "The fault, dear Brutus, lies not in our stars but in ourselves that we are underlings." *Marlowe.* *John Donne:* "No man is an island unto himself." *Diderot.* *Hobbes.* *Galileo.* *Voltaire:* "War is the greatest of all crimes and yet there is no aggressor who does not color his crimes with the pretext of justice." *Bruno. Descartes. Vico. Justus Lipsius,* who in the first half of the seventeenth century spoke of America as "the sun of a new empire arising in the West." *Montaigne. Gassendi. Juan de Mariana:* "It is a salutory reflection that princes have been persuaded that if they oppress the state they can be killed not only justly but with praise and glory." *Spinoza. Pascal. Holbach. Helvetius. George Buchanan:* "The sole source of political power, under God, is the people." *Grotius:* "Some writers have advanced a doctrine which can never be admitted, that the law of nations authorizes one power to commence hostilities against another whose increasing greatness awakes her alarm." *Duplessis-Mornay:* "The function of the king is to maintain the law, positive, natural, and divine; he is the instrument, not the dictator of the law. . . . Subjects, considered in a body, ought to be esteemed absolute lords and owners of the kingdom." And the great Moravian bishop *John Comenius,* scholar and educator who shortly after 1600 wrote words many have not yet taken to heart:

> We are all citizens of one world, we are all of one blood. To hate a man because he was born in another country, because he speaks a different language, or because he takes a different view on this subject or that, is a great folly. Desist, I implore you, for we are all equally human. . . . Let us have but one end in view, the welfare of humanity; and let us put aside all selfishness in considerations of language, nationality, or religion.

These men were rebels, rebels against entrenched, unreasoning authority, advocates of individuality and equality in the original sense of the words. Each helped ignite the spark that started the American Revolution, helped fire the "shot heard round the world" at Lexington. For as Gustave Le Bon observed:

> The philosophers who evolve ideas have long since returned to dust, when the fruit of their reflections ends by triumphing. . . . There are great difficulties in the way of establishing a general belief, but when it is definitely implanted its power for a long time to come is invincible. . . . When by various processes an idea has ended by penetrating into the minds of crowds, it possesses an irresistible power, and brings about a series of effects, opposition to which is invincible.

The great tragedy of the Renaissance was what happened to it overseas at the hands of the English. The submergence of the concept of equality and individual liberty as far as others were concerned occurred under a massive onslaught of industrial abuses, unbounded nationalism and rampant imperialism. The "greed and envy" discussed by Thomas Callander culminated in two horrendous world wars. One cannot ignore the refusal to extend to others abroad the democratic principle that the English succeeded to an unprecedented degree in applying to themselves at home, a process that evoked admiration all the way from Voltaire to Hitler, that moved the American magazine *The Forum* to state in 1894: "It should never be forgotten, even by the most ardent enemies of an aristocracy, that England today is the most democratic country of the universe, the country in which the rights of the individual are most respected, and in which the individual possesses the most liberty."

One can trace the *external* abandoning of the democratic principle by the English in their failure to hold the American colonies, in the paralyzing fear engendered in the upper classes by the French Revolution, in Edward VII's disgust when, as Prince of Wales, he visited India in the late nineteenth century and witnessed the patronizing attitude of the colonials toward the natives, in Kenyatta's resentment at

British superiority, in Churchill's disdain of Gandhi and his comment on the universally minded Sir Stafford Cripps, "There but for the grace of God goes God," in what is still happening in Northern Ireland, Rhodesia and other isolated parts of the world.

A later-day parallel may be seen in the sorry state of the American image abroad, a state of affairs which makes a mockery of Jefferson's declaration that "The American Revolution is for everybody," of Nixon's presumptuous reaffirmation in January 1971 that "America is the hope of the world." One cannot look toward any point of the compass without finding a desolate picture. The United States appears to be losing the non-Communist world by default. It is not a question of communism "winning." It is a question of the American democratic principle having lost all significance overseas. What we are witnessing is the fallacy of the idea that anything as "religious" in its profundity as the belief that all men are created free and equal can be limited to only a portion of mankind. At home *or* abroad. There is a fundamental contradictory hurdle raised that cannot be cleared by the most adroit of rope-skippers.

The enduring meaning of "The American Revolution is for everybody" was clarified by Dr. Martin Luther King in his resolution adopted by the Southern Christian Leadership Conference in 1967 which linked together the "End of the Vietnam War" with the drive for social justice at home:

> To win the world to the cause of freedom this nation must practice at home what it preaches abroad. The freedom which we seek in this land can be made a reality abroad only by its application to every ghetto dweller in America, to every tenant farmer in the South, for every American whether he be white or black. Nor do we believe that we can for long tell Americans to practice non-violence at home while our nation is practicing the very essence of violence abroad in this mor-

ally and politically unjust war. . . . Our primary thrust is still to secure equal rights for all men in this land. Rather than have the American dream slain in the jungles and swamps of Vietnam, we pledge ourselves to do everything in our power to end that war.

It is little wonder that Dr. King was also crucified before he was deified.

12

I believe it must be the policy of the United States to
support free peoples who are resisting attempted
subjugation by armed minorities or by outside pressures.
—The Truman Doctrine, Waco, Texas, March 12, 1946

IN 1969 another early Nixon appointee, Governor Nelson
Rockefeller of New York, after an official fact-finding tour
of South America, arrived at extremely pessimistic conclusions. A specialist in Western Hemispheric affairs for many
years before seeking public office, Rockefeller, in a report
submitted on December 9 of that year, stated that the United
States had allowed the special relationships always enjoyed
with South American countries to "deteriorate badly."

All these nations had become a "tempting target for Communist subversion." It was "evident that such subversion is a
reality today with alarming potential." Noting that the
present population of 250 million would rise in another
thirty years to 642 million, Governor Rockefeller concluded
that if this anti-American trend continued, "One can fore-
see a time when the United States will be politically and
morally isolated from part or much of the Western Hemisphere."

Chile and Venezuela were not visited by Rockefeller because of fears of riots. Peru was bypassed because of oil expropriation problems. During the course of the Governor's trip, Dr. Gabriel Valdes, then Finance Minister of Chile, called at the White House and presented the Chief Executive with the Vina del Mar report signed by twenty-one Latin American countries. The report concluded: "Private investments have meant, and mean today, for South America that the amounts that leave our continent are many times higher than those that are invested in it. South American leaders are convinced that South America gives more than it receives."

The following week President Lleras Restrepo of Colombia issued a strong supporting statement claiming that the exploitation of South American natural resources by "North American monopolies" took more out than was given by U.S. aid measures and that a total revision of United States trade and economic policies was essential.

Since 1969 the trend toward U.S. political and moral isolation in our sister continent has spiraled at an alarming rate. There has been no significant revision in trade and economic policies. U.S. taxpayers put up foreign-aid money. U.S. private industries take out enormous profits. The peoples of the two continents end up further alienated from one another.

Many of our Latin American problems stem from declarations made by John Foster Dulles in 1954 and President Eisenhower in 1960. As Secretary of State, Mr. Dulles proclaimed at the Inter-American Conference in Caracas that among the most fundamental of U.S. policies was an objection to the existence of Communist or pro-Communist governments in the Americas, even if freely elected. Six years later Eisenhower warned that the United States would consider it an intervention in the internal affairs of another country if any power was seen to support "subversive ele-

ments in that country." The two declarations pinned down
the Truman Doctrine in specific terms to Latin America.

"Subversive elements," "pro-Communist," "free peoples,"
"armed minorities." These phrases, which are open to interpretation in the friendliest of living-room discussions, have
served time and again during the past decade as handy ex-
cuses for the U.S.A. to aid and abet, encourage and insti-
gate repression, unbridled dictatorships and armed thuggery
in support of fascism that would have Thomas Jefferson,
Abraham Lincoln and Theodore Roosevelt wringing their
hands in despair. We have accelerated, not arrested, the
growth of communism in the minds and hearts of our
southern neighbors. Today they are far more anti-American
than they are pro-Communist.

Recently I spent a long weekend with a down-to-earth
Roman Catholic priest, considerably right of center, who
has served for eight years as a missionary in Peru. He stated
flatly that unless the present course of events is swiftly and
drastically changed, both the United States and the Roman
Catholic Church will be "out, finished, washed up in South
America." (A young Irish missionary home on holidays in
Ireland last Christmas after five years in the Philippines
stated categorically that the same thing was true in that part
of the world.)

It should be a surprise to no one reasonably abreast of
developments in South America that the Reverend Camilo
Torres, Colombian guerrilla priest gunned down by troops
in 1966, has become a hero of gigantic stature throughout
the continent, his words cherished by millions:

> In Catholicism the main principle is love for one's fellow
> man. "He who loves his fellow man fulfills the law." For this
> love to be genuine, it must seek to be effective. If beneficence,
> alms, the few tuition-free schools, the few housing projects—
> in general, what is known as "charity"—do not succeed in

feeding the hungry majority, clothing the naked, or teaching the unschooled masses, we must seek effective means to achieve the well-being of these majorities.

What has happened throughout Latin America—and it is more or less true right around this troubled planet—is that "subversive elements" have become synonymous with anyone who is in opposition to any entrenched reactionary government, no matter who are in that government, what they believe in and by what methods they become and stay entrenched. All one has to do is proclaim "We are anti-Communist, we are for the U.S.A." and the Tommy guns, the police batons, the napalm, jets and helicopters, along with the dollars, start to flow. One is faced with

QUESTION: "Is there no middle ground in underdeveloped countries between communism and fascism?"

ANSWER: "If there is, the U.S. Government hasn't found it."

Now that the North American Indians have been nearly decimated we embrace the survivors to our conscience-stricken bosoms, glorify them in TV Westerns, cautiously champion their forlorn causes. In the meantime we close our eyes to what we are helping to do to the Indians of South America. A panel of European doctors who, on behalf of the International Committee of the Red Cross, traveled more than 12,000 miles through the back country of Brazil in 1970, surveying conditions among twenty of the known thirty tribes, estimated that compared to the half million Indians alive at the turn of the century, today there are fewer than 60,000. They concluded that "without massive international assistance," the Indians in that country will rapidly vanish. "The general law of the survival of the fittest rules," the panel's report stated. Indian contracts are primarily with collectors of rubber, nuts and palm fibers, mineral prospectors, merchants, missionaries and "pacification" teams. "Some of these might be considered to be representative of our civilization, but it is important to note that others definitely cannot be regarded as such."

Throughout South America it is not just the Indians who are losing out. Except for a tiny percentage at the top, everybody is losing out. No more depressing picture has emerged than Malcolm W. Browne's report in the New York *Times* on April 3, 1971, as to how things are in Buenaventura, Colombia's only important Pacific seaport:

> The equatorial sun burns through the jungle vapor shrouding this shabby port, and men seek shade in open-sided saloons, drinking powerful aguardiente while they curse the Government and the Americans.
>
> Though enormous riches in oil, coffee, cotton, sugar and frozen shrimp pass through every day, the wealth never seems to rub off on Buenaventura, nor has it in the past. Unemployment is estimated at 80%, and theft and prostitution are the two most conspicuous forms of livelihood. . . . The main Roman Catholic church, solidly built of concrete, stands impressively on a hill facing bars, cafes and brothel hotels, all of which have neon signs. . . . The bulk of Buenaventura is a wilderness of wooden and sheet-metal shacks, skeletal dogs and raggedly dressed children playing in the dust. The shacks and squalor recede into swamp and dense jungle, dotted every few dozen miles by clusters of thatched huts that are as isolated from the modern world as any community on earth.

The Roman Catholic bishop of Buenaventura, the Most Reverend Gerardo Valencia, a member of the Golconda Group whose aims include "the end of United States capitalist imperialism," explains:

> In the Buenaventura region, 90% of the population is black, descendants of the slaves brought here many generations ago. These people still live essentially as slaves, working for the handful of white landowners. . . .

We believe, as did Father Camilo, in the equality of all men and in the rights of men. We are devoted to the struggle against capitalist imperialism and for a fundamental change in the Colombian system. Democracy has no meaning if there is no justice for the poor and elections are won by fraud.

Violence and repression centered last winter around Del Valle University, 105 miles inland at Cali, where, after thirty-eight students were apparently killed by gunfire, the university rector resigned. One student interviewed by Browne stated:

Our main quarrel is with gringo [U.S.] imperialism. Yankee aid is spent on our universities not for the benefit of the Colombian population but to produce technicians to operate the gringo-owned factories. . . . Furthermore, the Inter-American Development Bank, which provides much of the money, lends to the universities here on the condition that the system remains unchanged. We are pledged to fight for change.

Colombia is often described as the showpiece of the United States-sponsored Alliance for Progress, but if the aid program has touched Buenaventura in any way, it is not apparent. Colombia's statesmen are aware of the staggering problems. Former President Carlos Lleras Restrepo has said: "Let there be no illusion about what is happening in the country. The nation cannot devote its armed forces and police to combating by force the cries produced by hunger, misery and abandonment."

Not far outside the world-famous Mexican resort of Acapulco, things are not much better than they are in Colombia. In 1970 a high-ranking U.S. Army Reserve officer, a long-time resident of that lovely Pacific Coast town, told me: "I could take you up to hilltown villages within twenty miles of here and show you mud huts where four or five families live in one room. As long as such conditions exist, the Mexican people will always be against us. They see us as part of the system. The threat of communism is a very real one."

The situation in Mexico City is, if anything, worse than in the rural areas. Stroll, as I have done, a few hundred yards from the new elevated motorway close to the International Airport and you will find yourself in Netzacohuatl, a dismal shanty town inhabited by 500,000 people. Thousands of destitute families scratch out like emaciated chickens a miserable existence in dust and squalor, trapped in another wilderness of tumbledown huts and patched-up, unpainted shacks. If this is part of the "free world," one might well ask: "Who wants to be free?"

On practically all counts Brazil is the pivotal nation in South America. Its land area is larger than Europe. With 90 million people concentrated mainly along the coast, the whole jungle-mattressed interior is a vast reservoir of natural wealth—oil, iron, copper, manganese, tin—probably the richest untapped deposits in the world. The key question is, who is going to benefit from this potential wealth, the Brazilian people or U.S. big business and a handful of the native population? To date the picture is not reassuring. While statistically the economy is booming, with Brazilian foreign reserves rising from $230 million in 1963 to $1.2 billion in 1970, during this same period foreign indebtedness increased from $3 billion to $5 billion. All of the consumer goods and growth industries are dominated by U.S. capital. Ten years ago the national automobile industry was almost 100 percent Brazilian-owned. Today it is nearly completely foreign-owned.

What is most frightening is that in order to try to lift the country up by the boot straps economically a regime of severe repression is in complete control and shows no sign of easing totalitarian measures. One finds even that classic pillar of the *status quo,* the Roman Catholic Church, taking an increasingly liberal position, one of constant vigorous protest, leaving the United States isolated as the single outside champion of tyranny. At the close of the April 1971 general assembly of Brazil's Roman Catholic bishops an official unanimous statement declared: "We observe that in truth the phenomenon of torture does unfortunately exist in our country and that in some circumstances is carried out in an atrocious manner."

This was in the face of emphatic denials by the government that torture does exist and backs up several sharp protests emanating from the Vatican during the past two years. This is not a question of guerrilla priests, of Father Camilos. Supported by the Dulles and Eisenhower declarations, the Truman Doctrine and powerful U.S. aid in terms of weapons and money, the army-controlled political bosses are taking on some of the country's leading churchmen— the Bishop of São Paulo, with six million population the world's fastest growing city; the head of the Brazilian Dominican Order, Friar Domingos Maia Leite; and the Archbishop of the highly industrialized city of Volta Redonda, the Right Reverend Valdir Calheiros. Archbishop Calheiros is charged with "personal subversion" for having sheltered four seminarists in his palace who allegedly were distributing "Communist" literature. He has also been accused of supporting twenty laymen active in a "left-wing" Catholic youth organization.

The true role of the United States in Brazil is veiled in silence, punctuated by assurances that we are maintaining democracy, protecting the natives from "communism," helping them to benefit from their immense resources. It is a tenuous, unpredictable situation, bringing forth such tortuous brain-twisters as the lead sentence in a story filed in Rio de Janeiro by Joseph Novitski of the New York *Times* on April 5, 1971: "Repression, a fact of life in Brazil for the seven years of military government, has been justified as a tool needed to rebuild the economy and the democratic system." Which was clarified further on in the same story by the remark of one powerful colonel: "Maybe we had too much liberty for a while. Maybe it was time for work without so much freedom. Remember, Brazil could not be allowed to become another Cuba."

Yet the Batista regime in Cuba when it was toppled by Castro was the most repressive in the Western world. Nor did the Communists take over Czarist Russia in what could be described as a liberal climate.

With total censorship of the nation's press, with massive interrogation of clergymen, politicians and civic leaders by army intelligence agents, it looks as though Brazil has got the kind of set-up some yearn for here at home. One further quote from Joseph Novitski's article will suffice to show how we are doing with the youth of Brazil: "Those kids are never going to forget that the police who used clubs on some of them were wearing equipment that still had U.S.A. stenciled on it"—a comment by a politician on the 1968 police occupation of the University of Brasilia, reflecting how part of the $1 billion direct annual U.S. aid granted each year since 1964 is being spent. It could scarcely be argued that we are trying to convince the people of Brazil that the American Revolution is for everybody.

Even among those South Americans most anxious to work closely with the United States, criticism of our present strategy and tactics rings out loudly and frequently. At the 1971 annual General Assembly of the Organization of American States attended in Caracas by the foreign ministers or chief delegates of twenty-three member countries, including U.S. Secretary of State William P. Rogers, the Secretary General of the OAS for the past three years, Señor Galo Plaza, former President of Ecuador, expounded on the prevailing sentiment. First stating that the present resurgence of Latin American nationalism should not be interpreted as directed against the United States but "simply pro-Latin American," Señor Plaza went on to explain that these countries "are becoming increasingly disillusioned in their relations with the wealthy industrial countries, and particularly with the United States." Plaza blamed this on "the declining flow of financial cooperation, lending conditions that are adding greatly to the internal debt, restrictions on market expansion, and difficulties in utilizing technology from the advanced countries." He concluded: "What is called for is large-scale multilateral financial cooperation from the community of developed countries, together with a trade policy that encourages development."

The only major development announced since the conference was the news received several months later, on May 24, 1971, that President Nixon had exercised his option to exceed the ceiling of $75 million a year set by Congress in 1967 on U.S. arms aid to Latin America exclusive of training. (Training includes special instructions by the FBI and Green Berets within the United States.) The President also recommended to Congress that the ceiling next year be doubled to $1.5 billion.

The New York *Times* reported that Representative Dante Fascell (Democrat, Florida), chairman of the House Foreign Affairs Subcommittee on Inter-American Affairs, had written to Secretary of State Rogers to ask why the waiver came in the last two months of the fiscal year, "thus avoiding Congressional review." "The first we knew about this," said a Congressional source, "was during a recent briefing on the big Latin American countries. One of the Administration briefers sort of let it slip out." The New York *Times* continued:

> Details of U.S. arms contracts for arms sales to Latin America are being closely held by the Administration. Officials insist that no approvals have been made, but they concede the waiver reflects mounting pressure for purchases.
>
> The Government is said to be contemplating a $30,000,000 three-year program to sell tanks, howitzers, and armored per-

sonnel carriers to Brazil, a loan or credit sale of two destroyers to Argentina, and the sale of ground and air equipment, including transport and training planes, to Colombia, Venezuela, Uruguay and Guatemala.

One finds it difficult to square all this with a "trade policy that encourages development" of our southern neighbors. Or to see how it helps prevent, in Governor Rockefeller's words, the United States from becoming before too long "politically and morally isolated from part or much of the Western Hemisphere."

Are we riding the wave of the future in South America or will we be swept out by it?

13

'Tis something in the dearth of fame,
   Though linked among a fetter'd race,
To feel at least a patriot's shame,
   Even as I sing, suffice my face;
For what is left the poet here?
For Greeks a blush,—for Greece a tear.
                    —LORD BYRON, "The Isles of Greece"

DURING the summer of 1971 I spent a considerable amount of time in Italy with Constantine II, the young king of Greece. In these dubious times it is difficult to tell when if ever he will return to his throne. One thing is certain: The exiled monarch refuses to condone the words and actions of the uniformed gangsters who, having usurped control of Greece, quite rightly number themselves among the closest chums in Europe of the Nixon-Agnew Administration. As the dedicated, well-informed king has made clear in several public statements, he will not return to his post until the constitution has been restored, free elections are held and all political prisoners have been released.

It is an incredible state of affairs, the successors to such staunch democratic giants as Benjamin Franklin and Thomas Jefferson, who both enjoyed immense stature on the Continent, cheerfully putting up with dictators that the rightful king of the country cannot stomach. A brief review of what has been happening in Greece reveals a total perversion of the original "resisting attempted subjugation by armed minorities" intent of the Truman Doctrine.

On September 25, 1969, the eighteen-member Council of Europe, which includes Great Britain and France, released a 10,000-word report castigating the army junta regime in Greece as "undemocratic, illiberal, authoritarian, and repressive." On December 12, 1969, Greece withdrew from the Council of Europe, since it was apparent that the council would suspend its membership until such time as "democratic freedoms have been restored in Greece." Two months later, on February 18, 1970, the United States resumed military aid to Greece, which had been suspended since April 1967, when the army had assumed power. This initial "token" resumption consisted of five American F-104 Starfighter jets unloaded at the ancient port of Piraeus. On September 22, 1970, full U.S. arms aid to Greece was resumed.

As has happened time and again on comparable issues, the legislative branch of the U.S. Government is at direct variance with the executive branch as to our course of action in Greece. In March 1971 the Senate Foreign Relations Committee released a report strongly criticizing present United States policy toward the Greek regime. The conclusion was reached that "rightly or wrongly, most Greeks believe that the United States supports the regime." The report said:

> The policy of friendly persuasion has clearly failed. The regime has accepted the friendship and the military assistance but has ignored the persuasion. Indeed the regime seems to have been able to exert more leadership on us with regard to military assistance than we have been willing to exert on the regime with regard to political reform.

As to what was really going on during the time when we had supposedly suspended arms shipments to Greece, the report stated categorically, a statement that has remained unchallenged:

> Greece received even larger amounts of U.S. military assistance during the three years and five months the embargo was in effect than in the equivalent period before the embargo was imposed.

Average annual aid during the embargo period amounted to $107 million a year compared to $95 million a year during the previous three years. Additional embargoed material accumulated in the "pipeline" which amounted to about $43 million in "excess articles" and $68 million in "undelivered military assistance." The Foreign Relations Committee report was especially critical of the U.S. Embassy in Athens and the American Ambassador, Henry Tasca:

> The embassy often appears to be more concerned with the regime's "image" than with the substance of its actions. . . . The general attitude of the embassy is defensive about the regime —quick to praise during the period before the embargo was lifted but slow to criticize now that the embargo has been ended and in spite of the default on its assurances.

One thinks of the thousands of Americans who died only thirty years ago so that totalitarian rule could be lifted from Europe. Observing the surrounding urban wasteland from the summit of the Acropolis in the summer of 1970—and there are portions of Athens not much better than the slums of Mexico City—meditating on the civil repressions which are driving thousands of Greeks into an extreme anti-American posture, I found myself at least temporarily convinced that Western civilization is sliding slowly down into a bottomless abyss, with the United States setting the pace and calling the signals.

The Nixon-Agnew Administration paid not the slightest

attention to the report of the Senate Foreign Relations Committee. Quite the contrary. The following month, in April 1971, U.S. Secretary of Commerce Maurice H. Stans arrived in Athens for a two-day official visit which was interpreted throughout the pro-regime Greek press as strong American support for the army junta. Headline emphasis was on Nixon's own phrase: "Greece's economic progress over the past few years has placed her in the forefront of rapidly developing nations." During a visit to the Ministry of Economic Coordination, Mr. Stans in another widely reported statement referred to Greece's "industrial miracle."

How completely our Government is out of tune, running directly counter to what is really happening in Greece, was dramatically pointed up by a message sent at this same time to the people of Greece—on the 150th anniversary of their War of Independence—by the leaders of the two political parties who in the last elections of 1964 polled four-fifths of the popular vote. This was the first time they had joined forces since the 1967 coup. The message declared: "We are voicing the thoughts and feelings of the great majority, almost the totality, of the Greek people, in declaring our unshaken belief in the democratic institutions. And we are stating this belief united, determined to devote all our strength to the reinstatement of democracy in its own birthplace."

Mr. Demetrios Papaspurou, president of the last Greek Parliament, declared:

> The celebration of 150 years since the uprising of our forefathers against slavery and for political freedom finds the Greek people deprived of free political life and human rights.
>
> As president of the last Greek parliament I can give the assurance that the Greek people and the political leadership shall struggle in unbreakable unity to abolish the totalitarian regime and restore free and normal political life which will

enable our country to return to the fold of Europe and the free peoples.

One month later the U.S. Assistant Secretary of State for European Affairs, Martin J. Hillenbrandt was reported to have told the political committee of the Council of Europe in Strasbourg that the Greek regime enjoyed the "broad support" of the people and that the American Government was satisfied that the torture of political prisoners in Greece was *not extensive"!* To which the former Greek Prime Minister, Panayiotis Kanellopoulos, replied: "I was not aware, so far, that it was possible, without free and fair elections, to determine the true will of a people."

One finds the executive branch of the U.S. Government flouting the expressed wishes of:

1.) The U.S. Senate Foreign Affairs Committee. (Presently Congress has voted to suspend military aid to Greece.)
2.) The eighteen member governments of the Council of Europe.
3.) The vast majority of the people of Europe.
4.) Constantine II, exiled king of Greece.
5.) The vast majority of the people of Greece.

That the United States, in the foreseeable future, will be "politically and morally isolated" in Greece seems inevitable.

Another outpost of equality and individual liberty in Europe—Spain—provides an especially accurate barometer as to how much the United States has changed in its political and economic views. Back in the days before World War II, the American Government and an overwhelming portion of the American public looked with revulsion upon General Franco and his regime. He was regarded as another fascist dictator who had assumed power through force and who belonged in the same hopper with Hitler and Mussolini. Today it is not exaggerating to say that the present U.S. Administration, the State Department, the Pentagon, the CIA and a high percentage of the American people when they think of Franco and Spain react along the lines, "Ah, well, at least that's one part of the world we don't have to worry about. Franco and his chums are our pals." And yet nothing essential has changed in Spain during the past forty years. The change has been within ourselves. Reflecting on conditions in Spain, as well as in Latin America and Greece, could Richard Helms, director of the Central Intelligence Agency, have had his tongue in his cheek when he told the American Society of Newspaper Editors and through them the public in the spring of 1971 that the CIA is "vital to the survival of a democratic free society"? Can anyone seriously believe that Spain, Greece and Brazil—not to mention half a dozen other Latin American countries—bear any resemblance to democratic free societies? Yet it is our arms and money, our diplomatic corps *and* the CIA that serve as the key, indispensable props to these repressive governments.

In Spain during the past few years the most significant development has been one equivalent to what has been happening in South America. The Roman Catholic Church at influential levels has been shifting away from the supporters of the *status quo,* leaving the United States in the unenviable and dangerous position of sole champion of tyranny. Mr. Helms was overflowing with praise for the astute foreign intelligence job being done by his subordinates. But is he or are they advising the Administration that we are isolating ourselves from the masses in lonely alliances with elements that are becoming abhorrent even to the Roman Catholic Church? Slow as the Vatican is to shift from traditional political views, they seem to be doing a better job of reading the handwriting on the wall than we are. They are learning that one does not successfully resist communism with brute force but by strengthening the free will of peoples.

That a widening rift exists at the very top in Spain became clear even to non-intelligence agents in February 1971 when at a meeting of about one hundred national representatives of The Movement, Spain's closest facsimile to a political party, one of Spain's leading reactionaries, Blas Pinar, called on the government to resign. Señor Pinar, another of the lawyers who appear to be playing a dominant role in Western politics, charged that Communists had infiltrated the clergy and the army. Once more the old wolf cry is heard and in this case it is extremely difficult to accept the definition of "Communists" as a remotely accurate one. What is actually taking place in Spain is a power struggle between the hard-line leaders of The Movement, the political descendants of the Falange party which for years served as Franco's chief support, and Opus Dei, the more enlightened Catholic lay organization whose members presently control the Spanish cabinet. To call Opus Dei followers "Communists" is at best a bad joke, and for the U.S. Administration to regard them as such is a serious error of judgment.

In addition to their animosity toward Opus Dei, The Movement leaders have been savagely critical of the young, progressive priests in Catalonia and the Basque country who have allied themselves with the local causes of the common people. As one significant straw in the wind, during August 1971 a Roman Catholic bishop came out openly in support of striking workers, the first time this had happened since Franco come to power. It was hardly a *cause celèbre*. The Bishop of Las Palmas expressed his indignation that city bus drivers hadn't been paid their wages since May. Yet the fact that the protest was registered shouldn't be overlooked.

Several summers ago I was cruising in the Mediterranean on a palatial 130-foot yacht owned by one of my closest

American friends. We were refueling at a dock in one of the Italian islands, with a sun-blackened, middle-aged native and his young son handling the operation. Some sort of argument developed, and my friend, well known for his edgy temper, finally bellowed over the rail, *"Communisto!"* "No! No!" shouted back the father, holding up a gold cross suspended from a chain around his neck. *"Non Communisto. Catholico!"*

"Catholic Church *Communisto!"* roared back my friend, by then purple with anger. At the time I thought he was a bit off his rocker, but since then I have discovered that quite a sizable percentage of America's wealthiest citizens share his views. I have had several tell me that Pope John was a Communist. In the 1930s and 1940s Hitler dispensed with the services of all but the most pliable of the clergy. Perhaps by the late 1970s or the 1980s the United States will be doing the same.

Tucked in beside Spain in the Iberian Peninsula is Portugal, another U.S.-dominated bastion of freedom and liberty that is literally held in miserable medieval squalor and servitude, its 9 million inhabitants crushed down in the dirt while those at the levels of power still exercise tyranny at home and in colonial Africa. With the British bowing out over ten years ago, all this today is only possible thanks to American and/or NATO hardware and money. If you advised the average Portuguese that "the American Revolution is for everybody" he would either laugh or spit in your eye. Most of the peasants are landless or through inheritance possess a few branches of a single walnut tree. Between 1938 and 1951 more than a million small holdings were gobbled up by the huge estates. Peasants work for only three months a year at 60 cents per day per family. In the arid Alentejo only one out of ten adults has the vote; the rest are unable to read or write.

In 1961 several of President Salazar's political associates expressed the opinion to two London Sunday *Times* journalists that if free elections were held, as high as 80 percent of the voters would line up against the government. Salazar was presented to the world as a mild-mannered, thoughtful ex-professor who ruled with a gentle hand. In fact he countenanced wholesale pillage on a scale comparable to what happened to the North American Indians, but in Portugal the ruling class was doing it to their own people, are still doing it in spite of Salazar's disappearance from the scene.

As in Spain, there is a strong ground swell of opposition to the *status quo*. Again, it comes from young, socially conscious Roman Catholic priests who are beginning to receive support from the hierarchy, as well as university students, teachers and members of other professions. In Oporto on February 17, 1971, the first priest to be tried for having publicly opposed Portugal's colonial wars in Guinea, Angola and Mozambique was acquitted in a verdict that came as a surprise to local veteran news observers. The Reverend Mario Pais de Oliveira, a village priest, had received strong moral and physical support from Dom Antonio Ferreira Gomez, Bishop of Oporto, who appeared four times in court on his behalf. Bishop Gomez is a sturdy ally and a hardy foe, once exiled by Salazar for his advanced thinking on the causes of Portugal's disastrous situation. A minor sentence of the popular "Padre Mario" had been expected as a warning to the growing number of young anti-war priests. He had also been charged with "revolutionary social views," but the anti-war issue was given major place because of the "current emotional atmosphere" in which "anti-colonial feelings are beginning to be expressed." Until Father Oliveira's acquittal, any criticism of the colonial wars had been regarded as treason against the state.

During the same week of February 1971 another popular priest, the Reverend Joachim Pinto de Andrade, with nine other defendants, mostly students, went on trial in Lisbon for "alleged conspiracy against the security of the state." They were accused of supporting the Popular Movement for the Liberation of Angola. Simultaneously armed anti-riot police took over the campus of Coimbra University, Portugal's largest university, after a two-day mass boycott in support of the defendants. Eighteen students were said to be detained in Caxias, a political prison near Lisbon.

As an indication of how the Vatican thinks the wind is blowing, as news of these events was coming through strict censorship from Portugal, Pope Paul gave an audience to guerrilla leaders from Guinea, Angola and Mozambique who have been fighting for over ten years to liberate their homelands. What we are witnessing in all these Roman Catholic countries is the emergence of the United States as a third force moving into the position formerly occupied by the Church. And in Portugal we are witnessing a growing appreciation on the part of many that the African natives in their possessions are after all fellow human beings, while the U.S. Government continues to act as though *neither* the common people of Portugal *nor* their African subjects qualify as such. If the United States continues along its present path, it seems very likely we will eventually be bustled unceremoniously out of all these places while the Catholic Church will continue to exert great influence.

During the past two years, as I moved frequently back and forth across the Atlantic and around Europe, keeping up at both ends with the swift movements of events through newspapers and other periodicals, radio and television, one fact beyond any argument became certain. If the President and Vice President of the United States—as they so often bitterly complain—think the U.S. news media are "biased," they should get on a plane to London and take a look at what is happening to the American image—not to mention their own—among those who in normal circumstances feel most sympathetic toward the United States—the English-speaking inhabitants of Western Europe. One might argue that this results from the "insidious poison" being pumped out by the U.S. news media, yet the most devastating material comes from foreign correspondents based in America. They are not impressed by what they see.

Some complain that there is an "international Communist-inspired conspiracy of the news media." More likely the problem centers around a remark once directed by Max Burns, retired president of Shell Oil in America, long-time chairman of the Oil Industry Information Committee, to a gathering of communications specialists in New York: "Good public relations consist primarily in having something good to relate to the public."

Conservatively, at least 80 percent of overseas news and editorial matter has been unfavorable toward and sharply critical of the United States and its administrators. Day after day after week after month. Most of the favorable material has been devoted to the words and actions of the Administration's opponents. No elaborate press briefings, no slanted or packaged propaganda, no two-way deals with the Heath government on interrelated "colonial" matters, no attempts to play up favorable aspects of the news—on either the U.S. domestic front or in regard to U.S. foreign affairs—can alter the dismal fact that America's public relations abroad have hit an unprecedented all-time low.

The cross-section of four or five editorials from non-English-speaking countries reprinted daily in the Paris *Herald Tribune* indicates—against a continuing background of news stories from those areas—an even more deplorable deterioration of the U.S. image throughout the rest of Europe.

All that can change the U.S.'s tarnished reflection in the minds of our overseas cousins is a thorough philosophical change in America's governing circles and a corresponding about-face in their actions. Not to mention an honest, straightforward presentation as to what is going on. The comforting feeling that the United States is protecting Europe from communism has long since been overshadowed by the dread that the Americans, even more than the Russians, may blow the world sky-high. This is true not just of students, liberals, left-wingers, but of countless "solid citizens," as typified by my London publishing friend who believes "America has become everything it started out not to be." His is not an isolated point of view.

After trying unsuccessfully for many months to secure some reliable data as to how America is doing public-opinionwise in Europe (the U.S. Information Service was one logical source canvassed without success) I decided to conduct a small informal poll of my own. It was the morning after the January 1971 joint Congressional prayer breakfast at which President Nixon, with speculation mounting as to what he was really up to in Laos, announced that "America is the hope of the world." I was doing some research at the Trinity College Library in Dublin. Two students hawking copies of an undergraduate newspaper at the front gate agreed to ask all who passed by whether or not they thought America was the hope of the world. When I returned an hour later forty-seven people, mostly students, had answered the question. Three had answered yes. Three had said they thought the youth of America was the hope of the world. The other forty-one had answered no, with comments ranging from the unprintable to such as "You must be out of your mind," "You can't be serious," "If America is the hope of the world, God help the world," etc., etc.

It was not an encouraging picture. Still, these were students. During the next month 100 people in Dublin, 100 in London, 100 in Paris were asked the same question. They were stopped by interviewers on main thoroughfares. Here are the results:

LONDON

Yes	7%
Don't Know	8%
No	85%

PARIS

Yes	5%
Don't Know	9%
No	86%

DUBLIN

Yes	11%
Don't Know	24%
No	65%

There was obviously quite a difference of opinion between President Nixon and the rest of the world as to who is the hope of the world.

I wasn't surprised—not after the merciless barrage of unfavorable news I had seen over a long stretch of time. But thinking back to how de Tocqueville, Wordsworth, scores of the finest minds of Europe had felt a century ago, of Jefferson's conviction that "the American Revolution is for everybody," remembering the enthusiasm Europeans felt toward the United States during my first two trips abroad in the 1930s, an enthusiasm that carried over into the late 1940s, I couldn't help but feel that as far as how our best friends feel about us, America has already suffered a tragic fallout indeed.

14

Ever since World War II the military power of the United
States has been steadily increasing, while at the same
time our national security has been rapidly and inexorably
decreasing. The same thing is happening in the Soviet
Union.

—DR. HERBERT YORK, *Race to Oblivion*

ONE of the most astounding aspects of current history is
that both the United States and the Soviet Union for some
time have behaved and are still behaving as though no such
element as nuclear energy had been introduced into the ancient pastime of making war. Each has practiced its own
brand of gunboat diplomacy. Incidents smacking of Fashoda,
Agadir and Sarajevo are constantly pumped up to crisis proportions. The two principal powers toss tinderboxes back and
forth at each other as though a sixteen-inch naval gun and a
half-ton aerial bomb were still the deadliest weapons in anybody's arsenal. Such a criminally careless joint approach
to world problems has helped create dynamite situations in
Turkey (which threatens to blow through the roof on any
twenty-four-hour notice), in the Israeli-Arab confrontation
(where the U.S. Administration's dual obligations to the
influential Jewish segment of the American population and

the oil-producing Arab countries has resulted in a saner course of action than in most areas), in a dozen less publicized corners of the Middle East where one chance spark could ignite a roaring blaze that would flash around the whole surface of the earth.

The Chinese, French, Belgians, English, Portuguese, Spaniards take their cue from the two big fellows, heedlessly poking up glowing embers wherever they think it might pay off in personal benefits. Those coping with the running of affairs in certain newly liberated countries seem ready to go along with the rest of the gang.

In spite of fancy talk from both major powers, spectacular grandstand plays, earnest protestations of noblest intentions, noisily publicized minute achievements, mutual accusations that the fault lies not in themselves but in the other chaps, no real steps are being taken to reduce tensions. "Live dangerously," advised Il Duce, and everyone who is anybody follows his self-destructive counsel. In spite of faint rumors under the surface that the world's leaders are finally waking up to stark reality, neither side appears ready to say, "Okay, we've *both* been on the wrong track. Let's sit down and start all over."

The consequences of America's indiscriminate peddling of lethal hardware all across the face of the earth, ostensibly in support of the Truman Doctrine, have nowhere been more tragic than in Pakistan. With China and the United States supporting West Pakistan and Russia throwing her weight behind Bangladesh and India, the international struggle for dominance has reached schizophrenic proportions. Going back and examining the comments of two of the world's leading newspapers at the time when the political and military leaders of West Pakistan had unleashed their merciless attack on East Pakistan, one can appreciate the responsibility the United States must bear for what happened.

On April 4, 1971, David Loshak wrote in London's most

conservative newspaper, the *Sunday Telegraph,* that the perpetrators of this slaughter were "the elite of Pakistan's rigidly stratified society, and the core of the military leadership which two years ago pushed the army commander-in-chief, General Yahya Khan, reluctantly into the Presidency. These men never believed in the democratic process that Yahya set in motion."

They did not believe in it because they are not democrats by nature, by upbringing or by belief, but autocratic, patriarchal and patrician, contemptuous of "the mob," more of the 18th century than the 20th. . . .

They were counting on December's election producing an indecisive result. This would have provided the most legitimate possible excuse for prolonging military rule.

Instead, it gave an absolute majority to one man and one party, the east wing leader Sheikh Mujibar Rahman and his Awami League. From that day, December 6 [1970], the generals and colonels knew what they had to do.

Comparing the military strength of the opposing forces, Mr. Loshak clarified a tragic situation in which arms provided for the worldwide support of "democracy" by the U.S. were turned against innocent citizens of a "friendly" country:

They [the East Pakistanis] had a few British Lee-Enfield rifles left over from World War I, but hardly any ammunition, a few "pipe-guns" smuggled across from Calcutta, where they are a favorite weapon of the streets; a few bazookas and maybe a few machine guns raided from Government armouries; and they had the 10,000 or so members of the East Pakistani Rifles—trained soldiers with some arms, but a poor match for the crack units of Punjabis and Baluchis from the West Wing. . . .

The West Pakistan army, by contrast, has been immensely

well-armed and equipped. Much of its material, jets, napalm, machine guns, a wide range of comparatively modern weaponry, has been supplied by the United States for defense against aggression.

Five days later, on April 9, 1971, the New York *Times* not only helped pin the blame where it should have been pinned but exposed another painful example of the trickery and deceit that prevails in Washington today. In an editorial, "Blood Bath in Bengal," the *Times* stated in part:

> Washington's persistent silence on recent events in Pakistan becomes increasingly incomprehensible in the light of mounting eyewitness evidence that the Pakistani army has engaged in indiscriminate slaughter of civilians and the selective elimination of leadership groups in the separatist state of East Bengal.
>
> A State Department spokesman conceded yesterday that "we would be concerned if American weapons were used in circumstances such as these." But he insisted the United States has no first-hand knowledge that such is the case. This is sophistry. Only last month the Secretary of State, in his annual foreign policy report, noted that this country had agreed to sell additional equipment to the Pakistanis "for their largely U.S.-equipped army."

It is fascinating to see Thomas Jefferson's word "sophistry" emerging in this context. What is most distressing and ominous about the entire dreadful chain of events is that all during the Pakistani-Indian conflict and since the setting up of Bangladesh, President Nixon has petulantly behaved, and is still behaving, as though he personally had been thwarted in his support of men (Yahya and his trigger-happy chums) who were battling for freedom and liberty, with Congress, because of their cutting off military aid to West Pakistan, and the national and world news media,

because of their objective reporting of the struggle, contrib-
uting to his profound moral and physical frustration. Never
has a gambler who backed a losing horse torn up his worthless
tickets with such bad grace and obvious resentment. Mr.
Nixon will not soon forget, or forgive, India's role in the
triumph of the East Pakistanis.

In Kusadasi on the west coast of Turkey, during the
summer of 1970, one of the best-informed couples in Europe
(he is an ex-U.S. NATO officer, she the daughter-in-law of
one of Britain's most prominent late diplomats), who have
lived during the past fifteen years in various parts of the
eastern Mediterranean, predicted without any qualifications
that within eighteen months, at most two years, all hell
would break loose in that part of the world. They are not
alarmists. They are accustomed to living on powder kegs.
They do not speak lightly. It was a carefully weighed opinion. So far they are wrong, but the unfolding pattern of
events since they made the prediction has clarified enor-
mously why they made it. While there may be a little time left
to remedy errors in other hot spots, in the Middle East mankind teeters on the very brink of a third, infinitely more
cataclysmic, Armageddon. Only an immediate summit conference of all concerned parties, sincerely motivated by a
desire for peaceful solutions, can stop the rush toward
destruction—if it is not already too late.

In Africa, currently shaping up as the arena where the
most momentous action of all will take place during the next
quarter or half century, the plain fact of the matter is that
the United States has already launched what can only be
described as a "colonial" drive, the true motives of which
are exploitation and profit, concealed under the somewhat
shopworn cloak of anti-communism. America is attempting
at the eleventh hour to turn back the clock in Africa, in
spite of the fact that the bulk of authorities on African

affairs state categorically that the clock is not going to be turned back.

The underlying reasons compelling General de Gaulle to cut loose from Algeria in the face of opposition at home that amounted to civil war should alone cause us to draw back from such a path, one that will inevitably lead us to the "quarries of Syracuse." In South Africa and Rhodesia the United States is helping to shore up brutal racist regimes that have been universally condemned by all branches of the Christian Church, by the overwhelming majority of neutral countries and by opinion leaders in both America and Britain. No matter how much double talk is indulged in, these two sister nations are condoning situations that are anathema to the whole Anglo-Saxon concept of freedom and equality. When the World Council of Churches votes to give financial support to African guerrilla movements; when the United Nations Human Rights Commission in February 1971 issues a report that lists in minute detail over a dozen specific examples of violations of human rights in both countries as well as in Southwest Africa and the Portuguese territories; when the Archbishop of Canterbury bitterly condemns what is going on; when leading clerics in both African countries are arrested on charges of "subversion," their files and private documents seized; when the Anglican Reverend Colin Davidson, on being deported from South Africa, condemns Britain's decision to send arms to that country as giving "massive moral support to a white racialist regime" and continues, "People are quaking in their shoes. The system is so evil it has the seeds of its own destruction in it. It will eventually destroy itself"—when all these things are taking place, how can we again be so blind as not to read the fatal words written on the wall?

As the self-determination activities of black Africa intensify, as they most assuredly will, what is going to be the role of the United States in Africa? If we continue along our present ominous path, will we not be pushed further and further into support of the entrenched minorities? If, for example, widespread, highly organized guerrilla warfare breaks loose in Rhodesia and South Africa, as it inevitably will, what will we do? Judging from our backing of Portugal in Guinea, Angola and Mozambique, we will side-slip in under the guise of containing "communism" and end up being the principal support of our embattled white brothers. In which case we will end up in a situation both at home and abroad far worse than the one in Indochina, which after all began as a "colonial" inheritance.

The U.S. money and arms that have allowed Portugal to play out to the last whistle her bloody, anachronistic role in Africa have been matched by a disgraceful undemocratic voting record in the United Nations, a record that has embraced not just the Portuguese territories but all emerging countries. In most instances we seem to be doing our best to prevent their emerging. Working in close concert with the Heath–Douglas-Home Tory government, we are doing everything we can to still the "winds of change" heralded a decade ago by Prime Minister Harold Macmillan.

Glancing back over the UN records of the past two years: The so-called Lusaka Manifesto passed on November 20, 1969, expressed the "firm intention of finding solutions to the present grave situations" in Mozambique, Angola, Rhodesia, Namibia (Southwest Africa) and South Africa. The United States *abstained* on specific votes re Namibia and the Portuguese African territories and voted with the United Kingdom *against* the Rhodesian section of the resolution.

Another resolution condemning all colonial regimes, especially Portugal's, for "continued refusal to implement the General Assembly's Declaration on the Granting of Independence to Colonial Countries and Peoples" was adopted 54 to 0 with 25 abstentions. The United States *abstained*.

A resolution condemning apartheid, calling for enforcement of sanctions against Rhodesia, etc., was adopted 56 to 0 with 22 abstentions. The United States *abstained*.

On March 17, 1969, an Afro-Asian resolution condemning Rhodesia, South Africa and Portugal was passed in the UN Security Council 9 to 2 with 4 abstentions. The United States *vetoed* the resolution, as did the United Kingdom. (A much milder compromise resolution was adopted the following day 14 to 0.)

A resolution supporting the "inalienable right to self-determination" of the people of Muscat and Oman, the Southeast Arabia sultanate, was adopted 64 to 17 with 24 abstentions. The United States voted *against* the resolution.

A resolution supporting the right to self-determination of the people of Spanish Sahara was adopted 110 to 0 with 5 abstentions. The United States *abstained*.

A resolution supporting the right to self-determination of the Island Territories and Brunei was adopted 88 to 0 with 26 abstentions. The United States *abstained*.

The United States, Britain and France voted *against* a resolution to suspend South Africa's membership in the UN Conference on Trade and Development.

A resolution condemning Portugal's actions in Mozambique, Guinea and Angola was adopted 85 to 0 with 3 abstentions (the *United States,* France and the United Kingdom).

A resolution affirming the "inalienable right" of the people of Namibia (Southwest Africa) to independence was adopted 96 to 2 (South Africa and Portugal) with 16 abstentions. The United States *abstained*.

A resolution reaffirming the right of the people of Papua and New Guinea to independence, calling on Australia to fix dates for self-determination, independence and "free elections under UN supervision," was adopted 72 to 19. The United States voted *against* the resolution.

A resolution deploring the refusal of the United Kingdom to grant independence to Muscat and Oman was adopted 66 to 18 with 26 abstentions. The United States voted *against* the resolution.

A resolution supporting independence for twenty-six islands and island groups was adopted 89 to 2 with 22 abstentions. The United States *abstained.*

Quite a record for a country which in 1976 will be thumping itself on the shoulder blades for having two hundred years ago "in the course of human events" thrown off the shackles of tyranny, expressed the God-given right of self-determination and all that jazz. It's right there, in the opening lines of the Declaration of Independence.

Has the United States in the past ten years helped one African country—for that matter any country in the world —to move in the direction of a more democratic, traditionally "American" form of government? If so, it could not be discovered.

The American Revolution is for fr4¢?dzxpq@!!.

In Asia looms the long-range question of how America is regarded today by the common people of Indochina. Do they look upon the United States as the "hope of the world," the nation that for almost seven years has been fighting to help them and protect them from communism? Even the most ardent hawk could hardly claim they think of us as altruistic, noble knights in shining armor. All the evidence points toward a distressing, rapidly worsening U.S. image in the vicinity of this longest war in our history, a widening rift which will force America out of any creative part in the destiny of these people. Thus a more or less unpremeditated, creeping involvement has cost us dearly on three fronts—savage dissension at home in America, dismay and anger among those nations in Europe and elsewhere who traditionally could be counted as our friends, suspicion and hatred felt by millions of natives in Cambodia, Laos, North Vietnam, naturally, and in South Vietnam itself.

Perhaps Benjamin Franklin was right when he said, "There is no such thing as a good war or a bad peace."

The figures dealing with the civilian toll of the war brought together by the U.S. Senate Subcommittee on Refugees, considered the most accurate calculations, tell an appalling story: During 1970 the number of civilians killed in South Vietnam averaged more than 500 per week, six times the number of American war deaths. During the last quarter of 1970 over 150,000 South Vietnamese became refugees as the result of U.S. and allied military actions. In mid-1970, of the six million inhabitants of Cambodia, over one million were refugees. In Laos, 292,000 of the three million population were officially listed in early 1971 as refugees by the Senate subcommittee, with U.S. bombings cited as the principal cause of these wide-scale uprootings.

Against this panorama of civilian casualties and wandering hordes of homeless families whose principal concerns are to avoid death from starvation and the open skies and the occasional cold-blooded massacre, the American Association for the Advancement of Science reported a systematic, wanton destruction of crops and hardwood forests that would appear to be specifically prohibited by the Hague Convention of 1907 which was subscribed to by the U.S.A. During the past two years America has been meticulously carrying out the manifesto which horrified so many of us when it issued from the cigar-clutching jaws of General Curtis Le May: "We will bomb them back into the Stone Age."

Returning from four years spent in Laos, Fred Branfman, an educational adviser of International Volunteer

Services, told in the New York *Times,* April 7, 1971, of interviews conducted during the previous year among 1,000 refugees from northeastern Laos and the four southern Laotian provinces through which the Ho Chi Minh Trail runs: "Each, without exception, said that his village had been totally leveled by bombing. Each, without exception, said that he had spent months or even years on end hiding in holes or trenches dug into foothills."

A twenty-year-old boy from Khangkai in northeastern Laos: "The bombing began first on the Plaine des Jarres, then at Khangkai. Everyone seemed afraid because we had never seen anything like this, and we didn't even know where the planes came from. But we knew they were jets because the noise was like one made by the thunder."

A mother of three, asked why they hadn't kept moving, explained: "How could we? We had to grow enough rice to survive. The children and grandparents could not live a life of constant movement. And we had to try and care for our buffalo and cows, our belongings."

One "leathery-faced" old man described what it was like in 1969 when U.S. jets were diverted into Laos from bombing North Vietnam: "The planes came like the birds, and the bombs fell like rain."

A thirty-seven-year-old rice farmer: "In the region of Xiengkhouang there came to be a lake of blood and destruction, most pitiful for friends and children and old people. Before, my life was most enjoyable and we worked in our rice fields and gardens. Our progress was great. But then came changes in the manner of the war, which caused us to lose our land, our upland and paddy rice fields, our cows and our buffalos. For there were airplanes and the sound of bombs throughout the sky and hills. All we had were the holes."

Forced out of caves and tunnels to try and grow enough to survive on, "there was a good chance they would be riddled by anti-personnel bombs, shredded by fragmentation bombs, burned by napalm or buried alive by 500-pound bombs."

A thirty-five-year-old man: "Me Ou was my mother-in-law. She was fifty-nine when she died on February 20, 1968. The jets had come over about 10 A.M. and she was hiding in our trench with the rest of my family. It was cold and she was an old lady. She decided to leave the trench about 3 P.M. to get some clothing for the children and herself. She went into our house twenty yards away. Suddenly the jets came again and bombed our village. She didn't have time to get out of our house. She was burned alive."

A writer fluent in Laotian, Mr. Branfman concludes that "In spite of all they have been through, the people we have talked to are relatively fortunate. They are out from under. Today millions of civilians in Laos and Cambodia remain under precisely the same conditions. . . . the purpose of the bombing becomes clear. In the words of Robert Shaplen, writing in *Foreign Affairs,* April 1970, 'to destroy the social and economic fabric in enemy areas' . . . we are . . . practicing the most protracted bombing of civilian targets in history."

All of which throws into sharp perspective a statement made by Father Philip Berrigan:

> We cannot ravage the environment of Indochina, kill ten civilians for every soldier, and expect anything but do-or-die opposition. We cannot fight the abstraction of Communism by killing the people who believe in it.

Far less by killing those who *don't* believe in it.

Whatever happens in Indochina during the years ahead, one thing is certain: to millions of simple peasants until the day they die the Americans will be the murderers of their children, wives, husbands, parents, brothers, sisters, relatives, friends, each of whom had his or her "own heart and sorrows," who was "struggling, with vision or with blindness," for the "infinite kingdom," this life which is "got once only, in the middle of Eternities."

They will remember us as the despoilers of their ancestral homes, their lands, their crops, their animals—the savages who hurled death upon them without their having any chance to strike back. The cherished Anglo-Saxon concept of "women and children first" has taken on a new and dreadful meaning. The best we can ask is that the Indochinese remember that during these shameful years there were millions of Americans who, though not made to suffer, were as horrified as they were.

As for the Russians and the Chinese, is there any single piece of tangible evidence to prove we must all be collectively insane that is more conclusive than the fact that during the past twenty-five years 200 million American citizens have meekly allowed themselves to be totally isolated from 200 million citizens of the USSR and 650 million citizens of continental China, both countries allies of ours in the last interhemispheric holocaust?

The inhabitants of all three countries with their respective satellites have had their foreign affairs handled by their governments in a dismal fashion comparable to the worst idiocies of the Dark Ages. So far everybody is the loser. As Lester Pearson, former Prime Minister of Canada, stated in 1969 while advocating a United States of the World: "The problem is not the creation of new states, but subordinating the sovereign freedom of all states to peace, security and progress. And we may have years only, not centuries, in which to succeed."

In an Oration Day address delivered at the London School of Economics in December 1968, Hugh Trevor-Roper, Regius Professor of Modern History at Oxford, brilliantly interpreted present-day China in terms of the past:

> Theoretically, the Chinese Communist revolution is a re-pudiation of the millennial history of China. Communist China has broken decisively with its past, loudly and explicitly dis-owned its long and splendid history. The recent "cultural revo-lution" has emphasized and exaggerated that breach. . . . But, in fact, what has happened? The inheritance of the Kuomin-tang, of the Chinese Republic, has indeed been rejected, but the older inheritance of the Manchus, of the Chinese Empire, has returned to fill the void.
>
> Today Peking is again the capital of the Middle Kingdom. Chairman Mao, like the Son of Heaven, is to live for ten thousand years. The Europeans are again the outer barbarians whom the Celestial Kingdom has no need to know.
>
> Such is the revenge of history on those who choose to ig-nore it.

One can only hope President Nixon's overtures to China will lead to a new era of international relations. On the basis of innumerable false alarms since World War II, one cannot be blamed for fearing that these actions represent:

1.) A trick play designed to get the home folks up on their feet in the grandstands prior to Election Day.
2.) An emotional blockbuster designed to divert our attention from the hard fact that no real efforts are being made to slow down the spiraling arms race; that, to the contrary, in the autumn of 1971 the tom-toms warning us of mounting Soviet power were never beaten so vigorously, conditioning us for an-other staggering defense budget.
3.) An old-fashioned power play designed to drive a deeper wedge between Russia and China.

One lives in hope, but "hope deferred sicketh the heart." In the meantime Japan and Germany, unburdened by crippling armaments expenditures, are out capturing the consumer markets of the world.

With today's earth shrunk to tangerine size in terms of pinpoint accuracy and numbers of intercontinental ballistic missiles, Russia and the United States are now in a situation comparable to, say, France and Germany fifty years ago, each having enough Big Berthas to destroy 80 or 90 percent of the other nation's population within half an hour—yet continuing to address each other in swaggering, bullying fashion, neither country certain when the other might let go with everything at its disposal.

Is this a farfetched comparison? Dr. Herbert York would no doubt consider it an understatement. This distinguished scientist, after playing a key role in the development of the atomic bomb, headed up the Livermore Radiation Laboratory in the 1950s, served in a top Defense Department capacity under both President Eisenhower and President Kennedy, was a special adviser to President Johnson and today is chancellor and dean of the University of California at San Diego. No one understands more fully than Dr. York what is happening in the nuclear arms race between Russia and the United States. We human beings have a remarkable and often admirable ability to sail along merrily through the most perilous waters without being too concerned about the dangers surrounding us. After reading Dr. York's *Race to Oblivion* (Simon and Schuster, 1970), however, one reaches the conclusion that our blithe complacency is based squarely on abysmal ignorance.

Convinced that there is "no possibility of stopping the arms race except by political action outside the two defense establishments," that there is "absolutely no solution to be found within the areas of science and technology . . . that we must seek national security through other than strictly military means . . . and urgently," outlining in detail the two growing horrendous temptations to "launch on warning"—i.e., to let go with everything we have as soon as an alert is sounded that missiles are approaching, or even to get in the first strike—Dr. York arrives in his final chapter at what he terms the "ultimate absurdity," a *cul de sac* which breaks down into two unthinkable but entirely realistic situations:

1.) "Ever since World War II the military power of the United States has been steadily increasing, while at the same time our national security has been rapidly and inexorably decreasing. The same thing is happening in the Soviet Union."

"Each of us has lived as the pawn of the other's whim— or calculation—for the past twenty years."

2.) In the United States the power to decide whether or not doomsday has arrived is in the process of passing from statesmen and politicians to lower-level officers and technicians and, eventually, to machines. Presumably, the same thing is happening in the Soviet Union.

In a year-by-year rundown Dr. York gives the disconcerting facts as to how, each time the annual defense budget has come up for review, the public has been subjected to an avalanche of alarming facts about new Soviet developments, many of which later proved to be totally or partially false. We have deliberately been misled time after time right through the past ten years.

Dr. York ends his book with a strong plea for all of us not to sit placidly by waiting to see whether we will or will not be hurled headlong into oblivion but to try to help shape the course of immediate and long-term events:

Just as our unilateral actions were in large part responsible for the current dangerous state of affairs, we must expect that unilateral moves on our part will be necessary if we are ever to get the whole process reversed.

It may be beyond our power to control or eliminate the underlying causes of the arms race by unilateral actions on our part. Our unilateral actions certainly have determined its rate and scale to a very large degree. Very probably our unilateral actions can determine whether we move in the direction of further escalation or in the direction of arms control and, in the long run, nuclear disarmament.

Conventional good sense urges us to keep quiet, to leave these matters to the experts and technicians. My father, troubled by my repeated trips East to testify against the ABM, asked me, "Why are you fighting city hall?" His metaphor is sound; the defense department is indeed our city hall, and it can be depended upon to care for its own interests, whether or not these are the interests of the entire nation. If we are to avoid oblivion, if we are to reject the ultimate absurdity, then all of us, not just the current "in" group of experts and technicians, must involve ourselves in creating the policies and making the decisions necessary to do so.

The technical facts presented by Herbert York, which not one authority of comparable stature has contradicted, have not caused the slightest visible ripple of concern among those in high circles, nor have they gained one percent of the popular support they should have gained. Now that the Russians have attained nuclear parity with the United States, our Government seems to be trying to keep us blissfully oblivious to the fact that we are constantly threatened with oblivion, while we ourselves seem mutely to have accepted the conditions in which we live, unmoved by the fact that a large share of the blame for the rat trap we are in must rest on the shoulders of our own leaders, many of whom are taking full advantage of the fact that we are indeed prisoners of fear.

15

Lacking a sense of honor, people no longer behaved
honorably but masked their behavior with fine words. The
old love of serious argument was debased into ingenious
dispute, by which the most despicable actions were made
to appear excellent. The old admiration for intellectual
prowess degenerated into a respect for a certain kind of
craftiness, the ability to advance a cause by whatever
means came to mind.

—C. M. Bowra, describing the influence of the
Peloponnesian War upon the Athenians

ON APRIL 6, 1971, a speech was delivered in California
that hit an all-time American low in terms of deceit and
intimidation. The speaker was Vice President Agnew. The
occasion was the annual meeting of the Los Angeles
Chamber of Commerce. The entire text is a classic lesson
in demagoguery, a masterpiece of falsehood and hypocrisy
woven through with not too subtly veiled threats.

Mr. Agnew started out by advising his listeners that
"The nation's problems should be confronted without distorting the perspective in which they are viewed." He then
deliberately set about distorting the perspective. Announcing that he did not "intend to stand idly by and watch the
destruction—wittingly and unwittingly—of the institutions

167

that have been bred in the seat of the American free enterprise system over the last three hundred years," he proceeded to rip those institutions to shreds. Not only were the news media, by criticizing what happened in Laos, an example of a growing American "masochism" that would, if left unchecked, "destroy us as a nation," but leaders of government, universities, churches, commerce and the professions were all part of the same destructive element because they emphasized the "negative side of such topics as the war in Indochina, military surveillance of civilians, J. Edgar Hoover's leadership of the FBI, supersonic transport development and the economy." A sweeping category of leaders and of topics. In short, anyone, anywhere, who raises his voice in criticism of anything the Administration is doing stands accused of trying to "destroy us as a nation." Said Agnew:

> The leaders in the movement to plead America guilty because they can't muster the energy to defend her, to downgrade her among the other nations and to topple, or at least drastically alter some of her most revered and respected institutions—all with the purest of intentions, I am sure—are to be found in positions of influence in all walks of life: the government, the university, the church, business and labor, the news media, the professions.

A fascinating phrase, "with the purest of intentions." These poor, misguided dupes are not the real villains. Behind them, Agnew continued, is a shadowy group of "radicals who would like to tear America down." Employing the tactics of Joe McCarthy, he did not explain who these "radicals" are, so powerful and persuasive they can corrupt some of the finest minds and most influential people in America. He just affirms without proof they are there, and some people believe they are there because he says they are there. Nor at any time does he tell us what "revered and respected institutions" our leaders are attempting to "topple, or at least drastically alter."

If those Americans not in support of Nixon and Agnew are dupes of "radicals," then the most enlightened minds in England and France are also being corrupted by these same insidious chaps, for they are far more horrified by the trend of U.S. affairs than are those on the domestic scene. Whether we like it or not, this is Hitlerian stuff, designed to play on the deep-rooted emotions of guilt and fear. People started out taking Hitler with his toothbrush mustache as some sort of joke. They have been doing the same with Spiro. Perhaps we should begin to regard him with deadly seriousness. Gustave Le Bon singled out "philosophers, thinkers, writers, artists and learned men" as the "cream of a civilization" for whom parliamentary assemblies represent "the ideal government." A society in which churchmen, educators, editors and publishers, business and professional leaders and dissenting legislators are alienated from the politicians running the country cannot long endure unless authority is propped up by tyranny.

When Frank Shakespeare, Jr., director of the U.S. Information Service, recommends that TV personnel up for jobs be "screened" to balance off "liberal" personnel; when Senator Proxmire complains that eminent authorities are refusing to appear before Congressional committees because of intimidation; when no strong voice of protest is raised at what Vice President Agnew said in Los Angeles on April 6, 1971, it appears obvious that our way of life is being threatened as never before. The "intellectual" community in America is being challenged by the Nixon-Agnew Administration and those lurking behind them just as the intellectual community in Germany, Jewish and non-Jewish, was challenged by Hitler, Goebbels, Rosenberg and assorted Nazi "experts" prior to World War II.

Mr. Agnew included in his list of those who would

destroy us as a nation those who dared raise questions about the "economy." President Nixon in his Report to Congress, as fully covered in the news media on February 1, 1971, predicted a "vigorous, orderly" expansion of the economy during the coming year. Two months later, on April Fool's Day, Sir Frederic Seebolm, chairman of Barclays Bank DCO, the international affiliate of the 5,000-branch Barclay group in England, was quoted in small type by a few newspapers as stating in New York that unless there was a change for the better in the United States balance of payments, a dollar crisis would probably develop before the end of 1971; that there would be some "very serious discussions before the end of the year" if the U.S. balance of payments hadn't improved; that the world could not "continue indefinitely" to collect and hold dollars. "Something will have to blow."

Although Sir Frederic did happen to hit the nail on the head, he was undoubtedly acting as a secret undercover agent for the "radicals who would like to tear America down."

As for those who sought to destroy us by killing the SST project, who were they and what did they say?

Walter W. Heller, University of Minnesota, former chairman of the Council of Economic Advisers: "If the SST is such a profitable undertaking, why does the U.S. Government have to put up 80 to 90 percent of the cost?"

Arthur M. Okun of the unimpeachable Brookings Institute, another former chairman of the Council of Economic Advisers: The Government's arguments are "nonsense and palpable nonsense. . . . What the Administration is saying is a little like saying that, as Vietnam winds down, we should start another war to restore employment in the defense industries and Pentagon."

Paul Samuelson, Professor of Economics at MIT: "We are faced here with a colossal economic folly. . . . Government subsidy of the SST or similar supersonic aircraft is at this stage of technology and economic development both an economic and a human disaster."

Richard R. Nelson of Yale University: "An intellectual scandal."

Milton Friedman, Professor of Economics at the University of Chicago: "I find it disgraceful that knowledgeable government officials should use arguments that are demonstrable fallacies and have been so demonstrated."

James Reston of the New York *Times,* also terming the affair a "disgraceful debate," wrote his own terse, timely paraphrase of C. M. Bowra's commentary on the ancient Athenians:

> The most serious problem in Washington today—because it affects most other problems—is the decline of honest argument. There has always, of course, been an element of propaganda in most political discussion, but now the techniques of advertising seem to be overwhelming the normal procedures of congressional debate and the language in the capital is more inflated than the currency. . . . The SST argument is only the latest example of the general corruption.

As for those leaders of government who are trying to do us in, one assumes Mr. Nixon's alter ego would include, along with former Secretary of the Interior Walter J. Hickel, two other prominent members of the Grand Old Party:

> It is immoral to blast innocent peasants from the air. It is illegal for Nixon to wage war with no authorization from Congress. . . . In Quangnam Province, Vietnam, Americans have burned and destroyed 307 of 555 hamlets and have put the survivors into concentration camps that we call refugee centers.—U.S. Representative Paul N. "Pete" McCloskey of California
>
> Common Cause is designed to help solve the nation's prob-

lems and revitalize its institutions of government . . . to bring
about a drastic change in national priorities until we build a
new America. . . . The U.S.A. is suffering from a national
nervous breakdown which continues to manifest itself in war,
race problems and the polarization of the country.—John
Gardner, former Secretary of Health, Education and Welfare

One poses a question: "Has the U.S. news media moved
to the left during the past ten years or is the present Administration sailing off into uncharted waters?" President
Eisenhower began his farewell address in 1961: "First, I
should like to express my gratitude to the radio and television networks for the opportunities they have given me
over the years to bring reports and messages to our nation.
My special thanks go to them for the opportunity of addressing you this evening."

Certainly he had no complaints. In March 1971 a letter
arrived from the publisher and executive editor of one of
America's largest and most influential newspapers. It read
in part (name of newspaper omitted by request):

> I can report, as far as the ——— is concerned, that we en-
> counter very little in the way of covert pressures. Of course,
> criticisms such as those of Vice President Agnew constitute
> a massive overt attempt to apply pressures to various news
> media.
>
> All levels of government, like other news sources, attempt
> to persuade and influence newspapers, but I don't regard
> these efforts as "pressure."

Those two paragraphs have been mulled over at considerable length. It is hard to conceive of the Government,
with its latent and sometimes not so latent punitive powers,
as only another news source, particularly when TV and
radio stations and networks have the same Government
holding over their heads, like the sword of Damocles, the

federal granting of licenses. Especially when, as in 1969, Dean Burch, chairman of the FCC, which grants the licenses, Herbert Klein, White House Communications Co-ordinator (a post that never existed before the Nixon-Agnew Administration) and Frank Shakespeare were rushed in as front-line stiflers and coercers, in that instance as part of the frantic effort to rally support for the Vietnam war in the face of the anti-war moratorium and mobilization marches. The "overt, massive attempt to apply pressure" certainly runs head on into the words written by a distinguished editor of the London *Times* many years ago when he contrasted the duties of the political leaders of a country with those of the news media in what has become a justly famous definition:

> The purposes and duties of the two powers are constantly separate, generally independent, sometimes diametrically opposite. . . . To perform its duties with entire independence, and consequently with the utmost public advantage, the press can enter into no close or binding alliances with the statesmen of the day, nor can it surrender its permanent interests to the convenience of the power of any Government.

"The utmost public advantage!" There is the heart of the matter. One shudders to think how much worse a predicament we would be in if there had been no free U.S. news media during the past six or seven years. If you don't believe it, take a look at what has happened in practically all the countries of the world—Communist and non-Communist—but not in England, where the words of the London *Times* editor have not been forgotten.

Going back a long step further: *"Salus populi suprema lex estum."* ("Let the salvation of the people be the supreme law.")

On September 22, 1971, at their fall meeting in New York, the Association of American Publishers joined the ranks of those who Vice President Agnew claims are "wittingly or unwittingly" trying to "topple, or at least drastically alter" some of our "most revered and respected institutions." The association stated in tough, unflinching language that it was in fact the Nixon-Agnew Administration and well-organized pressure groups who posed a serious threat to one of the cornerstones of those institutions, the freedoms guaranteed by the First Amendment to the Constitution. "It is a critical fact that we are now faced with the necessity of defending the First Amendment," declared the association's chairman, W. Bradford Wiley. "Nothing like this has happened since the days of Senator Joseph McCarthy."

Kenneth D. McCormick, Doubleday vice president and chairman of the association's Freedom to Read Committee, reporting that pressures on school and public libraries were no longer limited to sex education and pornography, stated:

> It is more and more the book that really talks about the war and gives two sides of it, that presents the race problem as more than an unfortunate spat between two regions, that presents the United States as a country that's been right sometimes and wrong at others.

John C. Frantz, executive chairman of the National Book Committee; Whitney North Seymour, former president of the American Bar Association; and Harrison E. Salisbury, assistant managing editor of the New York *Times,* also voiced deep concern at the encroachments by those who look on Mr. Agnew as their inspired philosophical leader. U.S. Senator Sam J. Ervin, Jr., chairman of the Senate Committee on Constitutional Rights, at the closing dinner of the meeting summed up how he, generally regarded as the foremost constitutional-law authority in the Senate, felt about what is presently happening: "If America is to be free, her Government must permit her people to think their own thoughts and determine their own associations without official instruction or intimidation."

On the same day that the Association of American Publishers was meeting at the Hotel Biltmore in New York, Vice President Agnew expanded in Washington on what he had said five months earlier in Los Angeles. Before a group of enthusiastic supporters, the National Security Industrial Association, an organization of defense contractors, Mr. Agnew directed his fire at political leaders who he believes are leading America down the path to destruction. Singling out four chief contenders for the 1972 Democratic Presidential nomination—Senators George McGovern of South Dakota, Edmund S. Muskie of Maine, Edward M. Kennedy of Massachusetts and Hubert H. Humphrey of Minnesota—he termed their support of defense spending cuts as "reckless and appalling."

"All of those gentlemen are well-motivated, sincere citizens," graciously acknowledged the VP, "but, in my judgment, they should be held accountable if they disastrously tamper with the national security."

The news media interpreted his strong attack on those who oppose the Administration's policies as a resumption of the bitterly partisan role he played during the 1970 Congressional elections. "We shall fight those who would weaken us in the Congress and in the public," warned Mr. Agnew. "And we will not let them obscure the issue of this struggle under such hollow rhetoric as 'reordering our priorities.' " The gauntlet was flung in the faces of those who, like Dr. Milton Eisenhower and his commission, John Gardner and scores of leaders in all walks of life, have been warning for several years that unless national priorities *are* reordered, the nation is in danger of extinction through "internal decay."

The attacks on the First Amendment go far beyond the attempts to stifle intellectual freedom. Can any thoughtful

American not be disturbed by the "civil liberties" disclosures that surfaced during 1971, a chain reaction set off by Senator Ervin, the National Broadcasting Company and the New York *Times?* While the Administration's publicity powerhouse tries to smear these revelations as "unpatriotic and leftist," who would have dreamed thirty or forty years ago that the day would arrive when he would read such headlines as "Big Brother Becoming a Reality in the United States," "18,000 Citizens Said to Have Been Spied On," "U.S. Admits Keeping Files on 25,000,000 People," "U.S. Passport Office Maintains Files on 243,135," "Sen. Ervin Charges Secret List Violates Constitutional Rights," "Stolen FBI Records Show College Campus Surveillance"? The exchange between the U.S. House Democratic leader, Hale Boggs of Louisiana, and Attorney General John Mitchell, after Mr. Boggs in April 1971 accused J. Edgar Hoover of tapping the telephones of Congressional leaders and of employing "the tactics of the Soviet Union and Hitler's Gestapo." should alone give us cause for the most profound concern:

> MR. BOGGS: "I ask that Mr. Mitchell, the Attorney General of the United States, have the courage to ask for the resignation of this man."
>
> MR. MITCHELL: "Mr. Boggs's attack consists of slanderous falsehoods and the most vicious kind of name-calling. Americans will be shocked that a reckless speech like this should have come from the majority leader of the House of Representatives. With total disregard for the facts, Mr. Boggs claims that the FBI has tapped telephones of members of the House and Senate. That is false, and he should know it is false. Let me repeat categorically: the FBI has not tapped the telephone of any member of the House or Senate, now or in the past. In comparing the FBI to Hitler's Gestapo, Mr. Boggs has reached a new low in political dialogue. He should recant at once and apologize to a great

and dedicated American and the men and women who have made the FBI the finest investigating organization in the world."

MR. BOGGS: "Not only will I not apologize but I am astonished that the Attorney General of the United States has so little regard for the Bill of Rights and that he continues to defend this incompetent man. I state categorically that everything I said today was true. I do not speak lightly. I speak very, very carefully."

A day later U.S. Senate Democratic leader Mike Mansfield came to the defense of Messrs. Hoover and Mitchell, declaring that he did not believe Representative Boggs's assertions were true. Within twenty-four hours, when presented with incontrovertible proof that a Congressional member *had* been bugged, Senator Mansfield swung right around in support of Representative Boggs and called for a full investigation of his charges.

Not long ago I reread Sinclair Lewis' *It Can't Happen Here,* published thirty-six years ago. It you don't believe we have moved a long way toward being something we have never been before, it is a book well worth perusing. George Orwell's *1984* came into the limelight during the spring of 1971 when Michigan University law professor Arthur Miller told a Senate inquiry that, with thirteen years still to go, "a proliferation of public and private dossiers threaten to make the specter of George Orwell's novel and its 'Big Brother is watching you' philosophy a reality." Senator Ervin stated at the same inquiry that people are concerned because they are "constantly being intimidated, coerced or pressured into revealing information to the wrong people, for the wrong purpose, at the wrong time." A former U.S. Army secret agent warned the subcommittee that "the United States today possesses the intelligence apparatus of a police state, a loose coalition of federal, state, municipal and military agencies."

None of these facts might have become known to the public if NBC had not first carried interviews with a number of Army agents who had spied on civil-rights marchers, participants in the 1968 national conventions and Senators opposed to the Vietnam war, including Senator Adlai Stevenson III of Illinois. This became startlingly clear in an interview Representative Ogden R. Reid, Republican of New York, gave to the New York *Times*. "The remarkable thing about it," explained Mr. Reid, "is that the Army's 1968 intelligence plan was distributed to 319 individuals . . . yet no one had the sense or courage to question what they were doing."

This is the essence of these encroachments on the Bill of Rights—"the sense or *courage* to question." What private citizen, let alone his elected representatives, is going to have the courage to stand up and protest if this sort of thing continues much further? The FBI itself, as revealed in some of its stolen documents, believes that intimidation is one of the strongest weapons to use against protesters. In his *The State and Revolution* Lenin points out that one of the greatest weaknesses in a capitalist society is that the average citizen "cannot be bothered with democracy or politics." If this is true in ordinary times, how much more so in an atmosphere of dread and suspicion where to protest, to object or to question may bring down on your head the accusation that you are subversive, pro-Communist, un-American and can mean that your own dossier will be combed over for data that will be used to discredit and defame you. It is hardly the way to breed a race of intelligent citizens, to produce the occasional Bernard Shaw, Oliver Wendell Holmes, Benjamin Franklin, Winston Churchill or Bertrand Russell among thousands of intelligent editors, statesmen, educators, jurists, writers and thinkers.

There is no room for argument that the mounting collection of "secret" evidence secured through "illegal" methods is a soul-disturbing question. No one has summed up more graphically what is at stake than Tom Wicker. In the New York *Times* on February 11, 1971, Mr. Wicker wrote:

> No issue of individual rights of such importance has arisen in America in years, if ever, because the Mitchell doctrine gives the federal government the literal power to eavesdrop on anyone it chooses, without ever disclosing or justifying to anyone—neither a court nor the subject—the fact that it has done so. . . . The eavesdroppers are winning, like Pyrrhus at Asculum.

From much of the foregoing it would appear that the Nixon-Agnew Administration is being blamed for practically everything that is wrong in America. If so, I apologize. One cannot blame Mr. Nixon for what he inherited when he was elected President of the United States. We had already suffered two gigantic blows—first, the assassination of two Kennedy brothers and Martin Luther King, which collectively brought despair to millions who saw them as the greatest living protectors of the democratic system, and, second, the crassest electoral betrayal in our history when Lyndon B. Johnson's sell-out of the American people convinced millions that the right to vote didn't give them the opportunity to choose between peace and war.

One can blame President Nixon, however, for what he has done with what he inherited. In his Inaugural Address Nixon awoke in at least the hearts of the millions who voted for him the hope that he would guide the nation onto solider ground, into less troubled waters. His two principal promises were that he would bring peace and that he would establish harmony and unity between classes:

> I shall consecrate my office, my energies and all the wisdom I can summon to the cause of peace among nations. . . If we

succeed, generations to come will say of us not living that we mastered our moment, that we helped make the world safe for mankind. This is our summons to greatness.

And:

> To go forward at all is to go forward together. This means black and white together, as one nation, not two.

If you turn over those two glowing promises and examine their obtuse sides in the light of what has happened since January 1969, you will discover the two jagged, sinister rocks on which Arnold Toynbee believes all civilizations eventually founder: War and Class.

As 1971 rushed headlong from day to tumultuous day the flood of deceit and bamboozlement pouring into the newsrooms of America and the outside world rose to uncopable proportions. The Pentagon Papers created a global sensation not so much because they showed how completely the American public and its elected representatives had been tricked by every President since and including Harry Truman but because of the Administration's desperate efforts to choke off the disclosures. Outraged eminent citizens such as Georgie Jessel cried out that the New York *Times* and the Washington *Post* were no better than *Pravda*. It became increasingly obvious that the Administration was accomplishing one of its major purposes. In the minds of a large portion, possibly a majority, of the American people to criticize anything the Government was doing meant you were "unpatriotic" and "leftist."

Skimming just some of the cream off the top:

> Joe Alsop, in a column reprinted and widely circulated by the Defense Department, accused Senator Fulbright and other doves of hoping for disaster in Indochina, an accusation termed "unspeakable" by James Reston.
>
> President Nixon with fanfare attended the funeral of Whit-

ney Young, late black crusader for social justice, bringing back into the news columns Young's description of the Nixon-Agnew Administration in the summer of 1970 as being "sort of like Jello. You really can't get a hold of it. It's what I call white magic. You know, now you see it, now you don't."

Nixon stoutly affirmed at San Clemente: "This isn't a police state and it isn't going to become one . . . as far as the subpoenaing of notes is concerned, a reporter's, as far as the Government's bringing any pressure on the networks is concerned, I do not support that." While all the time his own henchmen were subpoenaing the notebooks of reporters and CBS films, tapes, transcripts, etc., used in the making of "The Selling of the Pentagon," and an Assistant Attorney General, appearing before a Senate subcommittee, haughtily announced: "Justice will vigorously oppose any legislation" that would restrict the "rights" of the Nixon-Agnew Administration.

Attorney General John Mitchell declared that the "New American Revolution" unveiled in Nixon's State of the Union message was going to be as "far-reaching as the Revolution of 1776."

A White House publicity aide called up Washington newspapers before the crucial draft-extension vote and advised that Senate *Democratic* majority leader Mike Mansfield was going to hold back funds from any party member voting against the bill, a report vehemently denied by Mansfield.

The President, indicating to Peregrine Worsthorne of the London *Sunday Telegraph* the wall flanking the desk in his office, asked: "Do you know what used to be there under my predecessor? Well, I'll tell you. A row of television sets. I had them removed. Politicians pay far too much attention to what polls, television, newspapers think of them." Why, that's one thing even his worst enemies won't deny him, that he is the most astute percentage calculator that ever made the White House. That's how he got there in the first place.

A real beauty from Mr. Stanley Resor when he retired as

Secretary of the Army on May 21, 1971, a post he had held as the top civilian in that branch of the armed services since 1965: Wagging his finger at the American people, he advised them with a straight face that they "must learn to distinguish between their roles in Western Europe and in Asia. The American interests are primarily in Europe."

When a bomb exploded in the Senate wing of the Capitol, serious, fair-minded European editors speculated as to who really set it off.

Democratic National Committee Chairman Lawrence W. O'Brien on Laos: "What do they think we are? Gullible dupes?"

The senior *Republican* member of the Senate's "powerful" Foreign Relations Committee, trying vainly to peer through the Laotian smoke screen, observed glumly to reporters: "Maybe the worst has happened. We don't know."

White House Press Secretary Ron Ziegler, asked by a UPI reporter at Nixon's Virgin Island retreat if the boss was being kept informed on Indochina developments, replied: "The President is aware of what's going on in Indochina. That's not to say anything *is* going on."

Senator Edward Kennedy commented that the Laos invasion had "significantly raised the level of deception at home. Soldiers were not dressed as civilians recently to deceive the enemy but to deceive us. The embargo on news was not erected to deceive the enemy but to deceive us."

The mumbo-jumbo surrounding the international monetary crisis convinced millions that Nixon had done something terribly smart rather than run the country into near bankruptcy.

The President denounced critics of his Indochina policies as "New Isolationists" who "have refused to learn the hard lessons in the history of tyranny," while everywhere we have gone in the world we have condoned, instigated, supported and encouraged tyranny.

"Lacking a sense of humor, people no longer behaved honorably, but masked their behavior with fine words. The old love of serious argument was debased into ingenious dispute, by which the most despicable actions were made to appear excellent. The old admiration for intellectual prowess degenerated into a respect for a certain kind of craftiness, the ability to advance a cause by whatever means came to mind."

The ancient Athenians never recovered from the disastrous effects of the Peloponnesian War.

16

The dice of God are always loaded. . . . Cause and effect,
means and ends, seeds and fruits, cannot be severed; for
the effect already blooms in the cause, the end preexists
in the means, the fruit in the seed. . . . Life invests itself
with inevitable conditions, which the unwise seek to
dodge, which one and another brags that he does not
know, that they do not touch him; but the brag is on his
lips, the conditions are in his soul. If he escapes them in
one part they attack him in another part.
—RALPH WALDO EMERSON, "Compensation"

DURING twenty-five years in advertising I can't ever remember being the slightest bit shocked by the fact that the
search for truth and the presentation of truth to the public
about the products we were pushing were of no importance
to the business. There was little that was unique about any of
those products compared to their competitors that *could* be
talked about. I do remember being greatly surprised by the
furor caused among the American people, the stream of horrified front-page stories that followed the shattering news that
the $64,000 Question TV show was rigged. Most of us in
advertising had known for years that many quiz shows were
rigged. (Just as we knew that only a small percentage of
testimonials were from people who actually preferred and

used the products they were urging others to buy.) Did the public really think contestants were as smart as all that? The best of them now and then needed a helpful nudge.

Anyone in advertising instinctively knows that except for a few visual tricks and different types of hawkers, the commercial bill of fare is never going to change. The same old balloon juice is always going to fill the air, the same old slices of baloney will always come out of the same old inexhaustible chopper. It has always been that way and it always will be. Advertising, once it goes beyond its original function of informing, has to do with illusion. And illusion and truth are two quite different things. Advertising, to be effective, must appeal not to reason but to the emotions, must play on hope or fear. It must offer the impossible dreams, the unfulfillable promises.

As far as both advertising and politics are concerned, one of the most significant studies of human motivation made in this century had to do entirely with this question of provable *facts* versus emotional *beliefs* or *illusions*. The results appeared in the *Journal of Abnormal and Social Psychology,* 20, 1925, in an article, "The Psychology of Belief: A Study of Its Emotional and Volitional Determinants," by Dr. F. H. Lund. The results were widely publicized in advertising trade publications and textbooks. They have been confirmed by a number of studies during the past half century, but this was the earliest dealing with the subject.

Thirty questions were submitted to 243 men and women at Barnard College, Columbia University, and the University of Nebraska. The questions fell into two categories—those that were provably true and those that were a matter of opinion or belief. In the first group were such questions as "Does two plus two equal four?" "Did the dinosaur ever exist?" "Is the sun the source of light?"

In the second group were such questions as "Was Lincoln an honest and upright man?" "Is democracy the best form of government?" "Should all men have political rights?" "Is the Golden Rule a practical concept in business relations?"

The first group of questions, on a comparative basis, scored +42. The second group of questions scored +88— more than double the first group.

The relationship of truth, factually provable evidence, to "desire," what the person *wanted* to believe was true, again on a comparative basis, scored —3.

Dr. Lund concluded, and other authorities concurred, that 1.) People's beliefs are based more on feeling and emotion than on reason or truth. 2.) People believe what they want to believe.

One can trace over the years and especially see all around us today the penalties imposed on the American consuming public by this emotion versus truth basic principle of advertising. The situation has deteriorated seriously during the past ten years primarily because, as mentioned earlier, Government agencies simply don't have sufficient funds to do a proper checking, testing and monitoring job. As one scans the consumer-goods field, from dry cereals and canned goods to ethical and prescription drug products, from soaps and detergents to automobiles (since 1967 over 12 million cars, 38 percent of the total produced, were called back because of "possible defects"), it seems incredible that sitting above the understaffed watchdog agencies there is in the White House a President who can stubbornly maintain: "Competition in American business is the best protection our consumers can have." It bears direct comparison to Herbert Hoover's 1928 campaign whopper: "The whole practice and ethics of business has made great strides of improvement in the last quarter of a century, largely due to the effort of business and the professions themselves."

In the preface to his superb history of the American Civil War, the Comte de Paris, the pretender to the French throne

who was attached as an observer to the Union Army, described conditions in the antebellum South in devastating
terms that can be directly applied to the present American
predicament. Commenting that "men who bought and sold
their fellow-beings took up arms for the express purpose of
defending this odious privilege, in the name of liberty and
property," he continues:

> This falsehood having become the basis of society, its influ-
> ence increased and gathered strength from prosperity. . . . A
> new school, of which Calhoun was the principal apostle, the
> teachings of which were accepted by all the statesmen of the
> South, assumed the mission of holding up the social system
> founded upon slavery as the highest state of perfection that
> modern civilization had reached. . . . Like a parasitical plant
> which, drawing to itself all the sap of the most vigorous tree,
> covers it gradually with a foreign verdure and poisonous
> fruits, so slavery was impairing the morals of the South, and
> the spirit of her institutions. The forms of liberty existed, the
> press seemed to be free, the deliberations of legislative
> branches were tumultuous and every man boasted of his in-
> dependence. But the spirit of true liberty, tolerance towards
> the minority, and respect for individual opinion had departed
> . . . notwithstanding their boasted love of freedom, the people
> of the South did not hesitate to commit any violence in order
> to crush out in its incipiency, any attempt to discuss slavery.

There is an analogy in what now exists in America, an
extremely narrow view shared by those running the Government, business and financial leaders and their hired hands,
the military, the establishment generally. It is reflected in a
common inability to look out at the scene around them
except from their own accustomed vantage point, from familiar, comfortable surroundings in which they voice opinions
and hear opinions voiced by close friends around them—
a narrow stance that leads to a blind defense of the whole

status quo because each segment, good or bad, *is* a part of the *status quo.* They refuse publicly to admit faults that are privately agreed to exist, standing up for flagrant actions by intimates because they are intimates, interpreting any criticism of our Indochina policy or a lavish defense budget or a tough, uncompromising anti-Communist line as a direct attack on the American dream, themselves, their friends, and the sanctity of the American home and family. They believe wholeheartedly in what they believe in because they too are victims of cherished illusions and, refusing to face facts, believe only what they want to believe.

It was another Frenchman who in a classic treatise first pointed out that in politics, as in advertising, people's beliefs are based primarily on emotion (feeling and sentiment), not on reason or truth, and that they believe what they want to believe. Gustave Le Bon, quoted several times above, in his *The Crowd—A Study of the Popular Mind,* set down in the early 1890s certain principles which proved disastrously successful when put into practice by Hitler in this century, which illustrate how dangerous and effective the Big Lie can be when told by ruthless protagonists in control of mass communications, with opposition intimidated and silent:

> Affirmation pure and simple, kept free of all reasoning and proof, is one of the surest means of making an idea enter the minds of crowds. . . . Statesmen called upon to defend (or expound) a political cause, and commercial men pushing their products by means of advertising, are acquainted with the value of affirmation. . . . To exaggerate, to affirm, and never to prove anything by reasoning are methods of argument well known to speakers at public meetings.
>
> Whoever can supply the people with illusions is easily their master. . . . Sentiment has never been conquered in its eternal conflict with reason. . . . Affirmation, however, has no real influence unless it be constantly repeated, and so far as pos-

sible in the same terms. . . . The influence of repetition on crowds is comprehensible when the power is seen which it exercises on the most enlightened minds. This power is due to the fact that the repeated statement is embedded in the long-run in those profound regions of our unconscious selves in which the motives of our acts are forged. At the end of a certain time we have forgotten who is the author of the repeated assertion and we finish by believing it. To this circumstance is due the astonishing power of advertisements. When we have read a hundred, a thousand, times that X's chocolate is the best, we imagine we have heard it said in many quarters, and we end by acquiring the certitude that such is the fact. When we have read a thousand times that Y's flour has cured the most illustrious persons of the most obstinate maladies, we are tempted at last to try it when suffering from an illness of a similar kind. If we always read in the same papers that A is an arrant scamp and B a most honest man, we finish by being convinced this is the truth.

When an affirmation has been sufficiently repeated . . . what is called a current of opinion is formed and the powerful mechanism of contagion intervenes. Ideas, sentiments, emotions, and beliefs possess in crowds a contagious power as intense as microbes. Contagion is so important that it forces upon individuals not only certain opinions, but certain modes of feeling as well.

Great power is given to ideas propagated by affirmation, repetition, and contagion by the circumstances that they acquire in time that mysterious force known as prestige. . . . Prestige is the mainspring of all authority. Neither gods, kings, nor women have ever reigned without it. . . . It is terrible at times to think of the power that strong conviction combined with extreme narrowness of mind gives a man possessing prestige. [Such a politician can] indulge in the most improbable exaggerations. . . . The affirmation is never too violent, the declamation never too threatening. Nothing intimidates the audience more than this sort of eloquence. People are afraid that if they protest they will be put down as traitors or accomplices.

Here we have a life-size portrait of Hitler painted almost half a century before he strode onto the world stage. And there are uncomfortable overtones in what is currently taking place on the American scene. Emphasizing our vulnerablity when confronted by demagogic, self-centered power, Le Bon observes:

> Isolated, a man may be a cultivated individual; in a crowd, he is a barbarian. He possesses the spontaneity, the violence, the ferocity, also the enthusiasm and heroism of primitive beings. In the realm of sentiment the most eminent men seldom surpass the standard of the most ordinary individual. The crowd is always intellectually inferior to the isolated individual, is only impressed by excessive sentiments.

When we examine the principles of Le Bon, holding them up as yardsticks to measure against what has happened in America during the past twenty-six years, it becomes clear that except for three brief intervals—the closing stages of the 1948 Truman-Dewey campaign when, under pressures caused by Henry Wallace's third-party candidacy, Harry Truman dusted off Rooseveltian idealism and promised it to the people; the swiftly throttled "New Frontier" Kennedy days; and a few months of Johnson's "Great Society"—the one profound emotion or sentiment that has been employed to motivate the American public has been that of fear—the fear of communism. Twenty-six years is a long time for a nation to live devoid of any profound, deeply moving hope. "Without a vision the people perish." At what point, to raise the question posed by Thomas Wentworth Higginson, does "common sense revert to the old safeguards" inherent in a true democracy?

Tied to the coat-tails of the fear of communism have been,

first, the assurance of greater social and economic benefits for all, which cannot be realized because of what we are told we are doing to fight communism; and, second, the assurance that by resisting communism we are protecting democracy at home and abroad, an assurance which, in the light of recent events and developments, is being seriously challenged in the minds of about half the American public, including most of the educated segment and an overwhelming majority of non-Communists outside the country.

Millions now conceive of the "hate communism" sales message as working directly *against,* in opposition to, the democratic principle which, since the founding days of the Republic, has been the most profound and deeply moving of all our ideals, the one sentiment of hope, religious in its intensity, which measures up completely to all of the Le Bon yardsticks. Time and again he reiterates throughout *The Crowd* that fundamental emotional ideas built around hope divide into two basic groups—"the religious beliefs of the past and the social and democratic ideas of today."

Boiled down to simplest terms—the emotional fear of communism has been used and is being used to smother and thwart the emotional hope imbued in the democratic principle.

U.S. Senator George McGovern put into words the frustration of millions of his fellow Americans on this score when he stated:

> Vietnam is just the most grievous manifestation of a world view that is based on what we're afraid of rather than what we stand for. I was a bomber pilot in World War II. I'm not a pacifist. I think we've now lost sight of the absolutely essential need for coexistence, even with countries with whom we don't agree.

It is not hard to put the finger on the super salesman who turned the American people away from the democratic principle as symbolized by Franklin Roosevelt in the 1930s, the principle which had united us with the Russians during the common fight against fascism but which was abruptly abandoned in favor of bitter, uncompromising enmity toward them. On February 5, 1946, at Fulton, Missouri, Winston Churchill, the architect of what was to be, presented his blueprint: "From Stettin on the Baltic to Trieste on the Adriatic an Iron Curtain has descended across the Continent." Truman, his enthusiastic contractor, speedily began to help with his doctrine to translate the blueprint into reality. Numbing fear replaced the exuberant hope that had been kindled with the smashing of Hitler, Mussolini, Tojo and their henchmen.

Overnight the world was divided into two hostile armed camps. The philosophical concept of world politics as envisioned by Roosevelt was hustled into the grave after him by his two supposedly most loyal supporters. What happened has been graphically described by D. F. Fleming in *The Cold War and Its Origins* (Doubleday, 1961):

> If there is a Third World War, Churchill's Missouri speech will be the primary document in explaining its origins. His was the full-length picture of a Red Russia out to conquer the world. Backed by the immense authority of his war record, and by the charm of his great personality, it preconditioned many millions of its listeners for a giant *cordon sanitaire* around Russia, for a developing world crusade to smash world communism in the name of Anglo-Saxon democracy. In print Churchill's battle cry became the bible of every warmonger in the world. It said all they had wanted to say and with his great name behind it, it could be used endlessly with great effect.

At the time of the speech the American people had not forgotten the immediate past. A nationwide public-opinion poll conducted several days later showed that only 18 percent of the U.S. adult population approved of the speech.

Some idea of the blockbusting propaganda weight thrown behind Churchill is gained from the fact that one month later a second nationwide public opinion showed that the speech was approved by 85 percent of the adult U.S. population. Never, in advertising or politics, has such a selling job been done before or since.

That the American people had not forgotten Roosevelt and the democratic principle, however, became clear two years later during the Truman-Dewey campaign. Truman nosed out Dewey, despite all opinion polls to the contrary, because the campaign conducted by Henry Wallace, Roosevelt's former Vice President and the Progressive party candidate, forced him briefly back to the FDR line. Despite the fact that the Republican party was trying its best to whip up anti-Communist hysteria, in the closing weeks of the campaign it sounded as though the President were murdering his pet brain child, the Truman Doctrine:

> The government of the United States firmly rejects the concept of war as a means of solving international differences. . . .
>
> We must continue to fight to assure full human rights and equal opportunity for all mankind. For my part I intend to keep moving towards this goal with every ounce of strength and determination I have. . . .
>
> I completely reject the idea that we should eliminate the New Deal. Instead we should build upon it a better way of life.

Those were the ringing messages of hope that, while the opposition gaped in openmouthed astonishment, hate foam still dripping from their lips, put him back into office. Two days later Walter Lippmann wrote in his widely syndicated column:

> It can be said with much justice that of all Roosevelt's electoral triumphs, this one in 1948 is the most impressive. For it

was the Democratic Party as Roosevelt transformed and developed it which won this surprising victory.

James Reston's column in the New York *Times* consisted of an open letter to his editor:

> The great intangible of this election was the political thinking of the Roosevelt era on the nation . . . and we did not give enough weight to it. Consequently, we were wrong, not only about the election, but what's worse, on the whole political direction of our time.

Henry Wallace, in the *National Guardian,* summed up the two basic emotional appeals of hope and fear that had been directed at the public:

> We brought the issues of peace and the New Deal into the campaign. Without us, the American people in 1948, as in [the Congressional elections of] 1946, might have had to choose only between two brands of reaction. We forced these issues, hammered at them, mobilized behind them until at last—point by point—the backsliding party of Harry Truman was forced to return to the principles of Roosevelt in a belated attempt to regain the confidence of progressive America.

At one point Truman electrified the nation by announcing he was considering sending Chief Justice of the Supreme Court Fred Vinson to Moscow to see if basic differences might not be ironed out with Stalin. At the time it created an effect comparable to the one produced by Nixon's overtures to China. Vinson was never sent, but the flame of hope was rekindled in many a deadened heart, and more than one hand that might have pulled the Wallace lever voted Democratic.

As for the one Republican President between Roosevelt and Nixon, in spite of all the magnificent things Eisenhower said in his farewell to the nation, it was, alas, a farewell, not a greeting. Fear, not hope, dominated his two terms in office. He became the captive of the reactionary wing of his party that had never wanted him, who looked on Robert Taft as "their" man. One is reminded of another passage from Emerson's essay on compensation:

> [The ordinary man] imagines power and place are fine things. But the President has paid dear for his White House. It has commonly cost him all his peace, and the best of his manly attributes. To preserve for a short time so conspicuous an appearance before the world, he is content to eat dust before the real masters who stand erect behind the throne.

Not that Eisenhower was content to eat dust. No man ever tried harder to get out of an assignment than he did the second time around, and no man was ever subjected to such pressure to stay in a job. He was able partially to restrain Secretary of State Dulles, Vice President Nixon, Admiral Radford, chairman of the Joint Chiefs of Staff, the Pentagon and the military-industrial complex, but in the last analysis he was owned by the hard-crusted band who have been running the affairs of the United States ever since the day Lee Oswald spilled the brains of President Kennedy all over the back seat of a car in Dallas. In the end they wore Eisenhower out. A sick man, he spent his final years in office playing golf, writing his memoirs, leaving the big decisions to John Foster Dulles, only telling his bosses what he really thought about them when he left the White House. The saddest words in the English language are said to be "It might have been." A fitting epitaph for a great man, ground down into the earth by those around him: "It might have been."

At no time do we see how completely the emotional fear of communism has dominated the minds, hearts and spirits of the American people since World War II than in the words and actions of John F. Kennedy. There is no point in discussing here what would have happened if he had not, long before his natural time, been buried in Arlington Cemetery. It is hard to believe he would not have shown flexibility in the face of changing conditions, that—like his brothers Robert and Edward Kennedy after him—he would not have drawn back from some of the dire compromises and penalties ensuing from the policy. Certainly with his human warmth and his unmatchable ability to communicate with fellow men all across the face of the earth, above all to be trusted by them, he could not have failed to play a major role in creating a different world climate than the stifling, fearful one in which we now live.

But the only relevant point is that President Kennedy did accept the basic sales message expounded at Fulton, Missouri, accepted it with a passionate ardor equal to that felt by Churchill himself. And most of us backed him all the way.

It has been since the assassination of President Kennedy that the trend of American politics has slowly moved outside the pale as far as a sizable percentage of the news media, the educated community and its leaders, the young, the black, the poor and our more progressive legislators (including many Republicans) are concerned. One can debate why this has happened, but no one can deny that it has happened. In all directions we see signs that the dread of communism isn't working any more as a unifying, emotional, motivating force. Instead it is splitting the country in two.

It is not difficult to think of the over-all U.S. current political situation in advertising terms. The public is the market. The client is the hard-boiled group of backroom boys who are in control of our destinies. Nixon and Agnew are the heads of the agency that has the account, backed up by their skillfully trained team of specialists—psychologists, research men, copy writers, mass-media experts. For some time the "halitosis" or "B.O." appeal they have been featuring has been "Fear of Communism," and the product they have been selling to overcome that fear has been a big defense budget. During the past few years more and more people refuse to be scared by the fear of communism into buying the product. Instead of looking around for some other appeal, refusing to turn to the hope on which the country was built, Nixon and Agnew are trying to pressure the people into buying.

The most bitter criticism leveled at the young of America by Spiro Agnew and others is that they no longer respond to the traditional emotional appeals centered around the love of one's country. In *The Crowd* Le Bon lists *honor, self-sacrifice, patriotism, glory* and *spiritual faith* as the "five sentiments that are the mainsprings of all civilizations." Which would seem to endorse our Vice President's high opinion of them. Le Bon, however, goes on to point out that there are historical junctures when a nation will no longer respond to the first four of these sentiments when they are invoked by the leaders of that nation. Confidence in those sentiments, along with confidence in those leaders, has been lost. Spiritual faith, the fifth sentiment, ceases to exist. He cites as one example the French monarchy under Louis XVI and Marie Antoinette. The populace had become apathetic, unresponsive to the tried-and-true clarion calls. The Government had forfeited obedience and respect. The French no longer believed their rulers or believed in them. Prestige had vanished. Yet those sentiments were not dead, only slumbering beneath the surface. The French Revolution a few years later represented the "establishment of a new *religious belief* in the minds of the masses" that rekindled four other "mainsprings of all civilizations."

"The striving of an entire nation towards the conquest of social equality, and the realization of abstract rights and ideal liberties, caused the tottering of all thrones and profoundly disturbed the Western world. . . . The world had never seen on such a scale what may result from the promulgation of an idea."

Given the new spiritual faith, the French responded to the sentiments of honor, self-sacrifice, patriotism and love of glory as never before or since in their illustrious history. The people's armies, little more than hastily assembled mobs, streamed out to the frontiers of their once more beloved country and beat back, under the guidance of Doumouriez, Hoche and others, the crack regiments of practically every European nation, performed flaming deeds of glory and honor, self-sacrifice and patriotism not even exceeded under the leadership of Napoleon. As did the Americans at Lexington, Valley Forge, Concord, Saratoga and Yorktown. As did the Russians on their own frontiers in 1919 when White Russian and alien expeditionary forces tried to hold them back from what they felt was their glorious new destiny.

Again in France one sees the booster process in action, as the democratic principle propelled the French on into the Napoleonic era, carried French armies all across Europe, into North Africa and Egypt, finally to ruin at Moscow. It was only when the spiritual faith, the emotion bound up in the democratic principle was submerged in a sea of lesser considerations that the booster process spent itself.

Perhaps we are at such a juncture in our own history. Public-opinion polls made during the past several years indicate that not only the young of America but a high percentage of the adult population have lost faith in our leaders, no longer believe or believe in them. On top of which all the signs point toward the nation's dissidents being imbued with a spiritual faith based on hope, not fear, that rivals in intensity the spiritual faith that motivated the makers of the American Revolution, as well as those who brought about and participated in the French Revolution.

They are inspired not by fear and hatred but by love, tolerance and brotherhood. (Note the specific emphasis put on *love*, not *hate*, in the preamble to the resolutions adopted by the White House Congress of Youth in Estes Park.)

It may also well be that those who oppose current U.S. policies have a far more realistic concept of self-preservation, the instinct on which the fear of communism is based, than do those who support the Administration. The young, born into a world greatly reduced in size, unencumbered as they are by our reliance on the comfortable, familiar material things about us that make for a feeling of false security, may understand much more clearly the full implications of Dr. York's statement that the "military power of the United States has been steadily increasing, while at the same time our national security has been rapidly and inexorably decreasing." In which case they have working on their side the unbeatable combination of the democratic principle *and* self-preservation.

Twenty years ago, in 1952, ten years after the dawn of the Atomic Age, in a preface to a new edition of *Foundations of Modern Art* (Dover Publications), Amadee Ozenfant wrote:

> Yesterday our dreams of the universe were one-way dreams, soaring towards the sky. Today our thoughts oscillate between two fabulously distant but homologous poles: atoms and stars. Today we think there is in the tiny dot that ends this sentence more organized worlds than stars that glitter in heaven. I presume that our school children in twenty years when their minds have digested the modern vision of the world, will laugh at the way our fathers saw the universe, as nowadays we smile to think of God with a long beard.

The youth of today have gone Ozenfant one better. After twenty years they are not only laughing at the way our fathers saw the universe. They are laughing at the way *we* see the universe.

Miss Melina Mercouri and Spiro Agnew's father were both born where the poet Byron, among others, believe it all began. On arrival in New York early in 1971, Miss Mercouri said, "You are close to the real thing—democracy. But, ah, right now you are not in very good shape."

I know nothing about the politics of the star of *Never on Sunday* and *Promise at Dawn*. I imagine she is on the FBI hot list. She is surely, unlike Spiro Agnew, not welcome in her native land, any more than Byron was regarded with affection by the tyrants who had Greece under their heels in his day. But best of anyone she has summed up the American dilemma. We seem so near to what so many have worked toward for so long. Yet right now we seem so far away.

On a lovely strand of white beach in Spain, facing the gently breaking Atlantic rollers halfway between Tarifa, Europe's closest point to Africa, and immortalized Cape Trafalgar, there is a tiny cluster of huts called Antica. It is the poorest village I have ever been in. Under a crazily thatched awning beside a shack that is collapsing under a rusty corrugated sheet of metal, six people can have a four-course lunch of olives, fish, tomatoes, salad, cheese and bread with six bottles of local dark red wine at a total cost slightly under two dollars. Skinny cats ravish what is left over. Pigs and goats wander across the hot sand from one shattered peasant hovel to the next. NATO jets trail threads of wispy white across the shimmering, limitless blue sky. The last time I was there two elaborately garbed soldiers joined us under the thatchwork, smilingly toasted *Los Americanos*. One of them led me behind a nearby hut, where, within the bleached wooden palings of a pigsty, stood four superbly fluted Roman columns.

Antica was founded by Italians, but centuries before them

the Phoenicians and Carthaginians had been there. In 1921 a Scandinavian archaeological team uncovered a splendid Roman forum between the village and the ocean. Foundation stones of an extensive town came to light. Today tiny glistening grains of wind-blown sand have reburied everything but those four magnificent columns.

Antica, like the Acropolis, symbolizes to me man's inability to learn the lessons of the past. We appear to be heading downhill again, not driven there by attacks from outside but because of internal decay. We are being led into the pit by the Pied Pipers who, ignoring the deep-rooted longings of their fellow human beings, go right on plotting their mischief and concocting their lies. As one partner of mine was fond of saying, "The facts that built a business are often forgotten."

A business—and a nation.

I must admit that I am a captive of my environment and my times. I often miss the familiar scenes and happenings of my younger years. I enjoy nothing more than to sit in the Yale Bowl watching the home team play Harvard or Princeton. I still brush a nostalgic tear out of the corner of my eye when an orchestra plays "If I Had You" (the Prince of Wales's—sorry, the Duke of Windsor's—and my favorite tune). I would like to chase a hockey puck one more time around the pond outside New Milford, Connecticut, where I went to school. If we didn't discuss politics, I might even enjoy eighteen holes of golf with Spiro Agnew and two of his Baltimore chums, followed by three or four ice-cold Pine Valleys in the locker room. When I started out twelve years ago on what was to be a leisurely pilgrimage around the world that somehow eased off in Ireland, I tried to sum up, in a speech made by the principal character in a play I was writing, how I felt about my native land. He too was starting out around the world, and he delivered his valedictory at the local country club before his old school friends and business associates:

October mornings lock their golden clasps around me in the stiffened fields and soft winds blow across the whispering grass. Sweet cider pines for many russet moons and clear the bells on Sunday morning chime. Full-cheeked the shiny bugle calls and oft the rustling snow creeps under backyard fences into cellar doors while ancient folk dream out their ancient dreams and lonely eagles race across the iron-gray prairie skies. The rushing stream dives down the steep ravine behind Chuck Edward's garage and ghosts of trolley cars still cross the T at midnight far away in Morton's Grove. Slowly the twilight falls across the measured tree-lined squares of lawn and roller skates re-echo where the last long line of blue-clad figures faded off into the mists beyond. No more will hurried steps of Orville Brown awake me in the restless dawn, milk bottles clanking somewhere east of Avalon. No more will cheery windows gleaming clear and bright across the hedges by my straight-cut classic door touch me like warming friendly neighbors in the dark. And so farewell. The beckoning alien corn arouses in me slumbering freedom's note. Remember me, as I will surely long remember you, until at length when all of us are gathered up within the gentle folds of everlasting night.

Yes, I am a hopeless captive of the past. But something has gone terribly wrong with the present. Perhaps we are going to have to stop letting the front-runners—the protesters, the young, the impoverished, the teachers, the outraged commentators, the blacks—fight alone the battle we should be fighting ourselves. Above all, as a nation we must stop telling lies, to others and to ourselves.

When we see the blood of women and children murdered by others staining our own hands, when we are haunted by visions of peasants fleeing from napalm and bombs, when we think of youthful bodies stretched out on our campuses not in quiet repose but in death and of old, poverty-stricken men drinking in shabby Colombian cafes, cursing "U.S. imperialism," it is hard to close one's mind and heart to the truth, to sit down with friends and enjoy a cozy dinner, sparkling conversation and a magnum or two of Richebourg '49.

Who knows, Ralph Waldo Emerson may have had you and me in mind when he wrote the closing words of his essay on self-reliance: "Nothing can bring you peace but the triumph of principles."